Contents

	page
Introduction	v
William Wilson	1
The Gold-Bug	10
The Fall of the House of Usher	25
The Red Death	34
The Barrel of Amontillado	38
The Whirlpool	43
The Pit and the Pendulum	53
The Stolen Letter	62
Metzengerstein	73
The Murders in the Rue Morgue	79
Activities	100

Tales of Mystery and Imagination

EDGAR ALLAN POE

Level 5

Retold by Roland John
Series Editors: Andy Hopkins and Jocelyn Potter

Pearson Education Limited
Edinburgh Gate, Harlow,
Essex CM20 2JE, England
and Associated Companies throughout the world.

ISBN 0 582 498058

First published in the Longman Simplified English Series 1964
First published in Longman Fiction 1993
This edition first published 2001

NEW EDITION

Copyright © Penguin Books Ltd 2001

Typeset by Pantek Arts Ltd, Maidstone, Kent
Set in 11/14pt Bembo
Printed in Spain by Mateu Cromo, S.A. Pinto (Madrid)

Published by Pearson Education Limited in association with
Penguin Books Ltd, both companies being subsidiaries of Pearson Plc

For a complete list of the titles available in the Penguin Readers series please write to your local
Pearson Education office or to: Marketing Department, Penguin Longman Publishing,
5 Bentinck Street, London, W1M 5RN.

Introduction

*'You have won and I have lost. But, from now on you too are dead …
You existed in me – and this body is your own. See how completely you
have, through my death, murdered yourself.'*

The short stories of Edgar Allan Poe are often strange, wild and
highly imaginative. Many of them examine in an extremely
detailed way the dark side of human existence. In his time, Poe
was a very original writer. His stories communicate a world of
terror that comes straight from the depths of his own troubled
mind.

'William Wilson' (1839) is set in England, where Poe also went
to school. It is a disturbing story about the struggle between the
good and bad sides of a young man's character.

'The Gold-Bug' (1843) is one of Poe's most popular stories,
selling over 300,000 copies in its first year. The story shows how
clear thinking can make sense of things we do not at first
understand. In this case, the clear thinking leads to the discovery
of immense treasures.

Another strange and very frightening story is 'The Fall of the
House of Usher' (1839). The character Roderick Usher has often
been compared with Poe himself; both lived in continual fear of
death and kept apart from human company.

Two more shocking stories in which death claims victory are
'The Red Death' (1842) and 'The Barrel of Amontillado' (1846).

'The Whirlpool' (1841) is an adventure story set on the
Norwegian coast, in which the main character experiences
terrible fear and lives to tell the tale.

'The Pit and the Pendulum' (1843) describes in horrible detail
the cruelty of human beings to each other, and examines fear and
hopelessness at the point of death.

'Metzengerstein' is one of Poe's early tales. Set in Hungary, it is a story about the power of evil.

'The Stolen Letter' and 'The Murders in the Rue Morgue' (1841) are mystery stories featuring C. Auguste Dupin, on whom other great fictional characters such as Conan Doyle's Sherlock Holmes were later modelled.

The American poet and short-story writer Edgar Allan Poe was born in Boston in 1809. He hardly knew his parents, who were both actors; his father left when Edgar was a baby, and his mother died before he reached the age of three. John Allan and his wife Frances took the young boy into their home and brought him up as their own child. Between 1815 and 1820 he lived in Scotland and England, where he did well in his studies at a private school near London. Returning to America, he went to study languages at the University of Virginia in 1826. He was an excellent student, but John Allan never sent him enough money to live on. Poe turned to playing cards for money to help him buy the books and clothes he needed, but lost so much that he was forced to leave the university after a few months.

Poe was determined to become a professional writer, against John Allan's wishes, and the two quarrelled. He left home and went to Boston, where he joined the army. In 1829 he left the army and moved in with his aunt, Maria Clemm, and her daughter, Virginia. John Allan died in 1834, leaving nothing to the person he had treated as a son.

Forced to make his own way in life, Poe managed to get a job with a newspaper called the *Southern Literary Messenger*. A year later he married Virginia, who was then only thirteen years old. He had begun to drink heavily, and problems with alcohol stayed with him for the rest of his life. He left his job and went to New York. He worked for different papers there and in Philadephia, and wrote and sold the short stories for which he became famous. In spite of his success, he did not always receive much money for his work, and he and his family were often hungry. Virginia developed a serious disease and, after five long years of illness, she died in 1847.

In 1849 Poe met a Mrs Shelton and they made plans to marry. He drank less, and for a time it seemed that his troubles were over. But the wedding did not take place, he started drinking heavily again, and he had no money. In October of the same year he died.

The first books of Poe's to appear, in 1827 and 1829, were two collections of poetry. These were not very successful, and he began to write short stories for magazines. The first collection of these, *Tales of the Grotesque and Arabesque*, appeared in 1840. In the years that followed, Poe became increasingly well known as a story writer, and more collections of stories appeared in 1843 and 1845. He also continued to write poetry, and in 1845 produced *The Raven and Other Poems*. 'The Raven', a cry for lost love, made him extremely famous, and it has become one of the best-known poems in American literature.

Poe's work includes science fiction, mystery and crime stories. Many of the tales are based on experiences of fear and sadness in his own unfortunate life. The stories in this collection are among the best examples of his writing.

William Wilson

Let me call myself, for the present, William Wilson. I am ashamed to tell you my real name, which is known and hated all over the world. Because of my evil life, I no longer enjoy the love and honour of others; and I have no ordinary human hopes or expectations.

I shall not describe the later years of my life, which were full of misery and unforgivable crime. I suffered at one time from a sudden tendency to evil intentions, as all desire for goodness seemed quite suddenly to leave me. Men usually grow evil by degrees, but I passed directly from simple dishonesty to the blackest crime. I want to describe the one chance event that caused this terrible condition. The shadow of death is over me now, and it has softened my spirit. I need the sympathy and perhaps the pity of other people. I want them to look for something in my story that might lessen the shame of my guilt. I hope they will agree that no one has ever before been tempted as I have. It is certain that no one has ever given in to temptation as I have. At this moment I am dying from the effects of a wild and terrible experience.

My family has always produced men of strong imagination and uncontrolled emotion, often of violent temper, and I am no exception. As I grew up, these faults developed and caused serious worry to my friends and great harm to myself. My parents could do little to change my ways, because they themselves had the same weaknesses, and my voice became law at home. Since I was a boy, therefore, I have been able to do very much as I liked.

My earliest memories of school life are connected with a large old house in an English village. I was a pupil at this school for five years from my tenth birthday. It was at that time and in that place that I experienced the first uncertain warnings of my terrible future. The full and active mind of a child needs no outside interests to amuse it; and my schooldays provided more real excitement than pleasure or crime have ever given me.

The unusual qualities of my character soon gave me a position of leadership among my school friends. I gained influence over all the other boys of about my own age – except for one. This one boy was a pupil who, although not a relative, had the same first name and surname as my own. This was not really very strange, because my name was a common one; in this story I have called myself William Wilson, which is not very different from my real name.

Well, my namesake was the only boy who was my equal in the class, and in the sports and quarrels of the playground. He alone refused to accept my opinions and obey my orders; and he got in the way of my plans at every possible opportunity.

Wilson's opposition annoyed me very much. Although I did not show it in public, I secretly felt that I feared him. I could not help thinking that my endless struggle to avoid defeat by him proved that he was better than I. But none of our companions recognized this; none even guessed that Wilson and I were competitors. I knew that he wanted to keep our struggle private. He did not share the sense of direction or strength of will that drove me on; he wanted no power for himself. His only purpose seemed to be to annoy me and spoil my success. There were times, though, when I could not help noticing that he showed a certain sympathy for me, which was not wholly welcome because it seemed to mean that he was sorry for me.

It was just an accident that Wilson and I started school on the same day; and, as I have said, he was not connected with my family in any way. But I was surprised when I heard by chance, after leaving school, that he was born on 19 January 1813 – which is exactly the date of my own birth.

Although I was always anxious about Wilson, I did not really hate him. It is true that nearly every day we had a public quarrel, and that he always allowed me to defeat him while at the same time managing to make me feel that *he* had deserved the victory. But although we could never really be friends, we were never violent enemies. It is not easy for me to describe how I felt about him: I disliked him, I feared him, I had some respect for him. But more than anything he interested me.

I soon realized that the best way of attacking Wilson was to make fun of him. But he was not easy to make fun of. In fact I was forced to make use of his one particular weakness in order to stay ahead. This weakness was his voice. For some reason – perhaps a disease of the throat – he could not raise his voice at any time *above a very low whisper*. I showed no mercy, I am afraid, in joking about this unfortunate condition.

Wilson got his revenge in many ways; and he upset me more than I can say. One of his habits was to copy me in every detail, and he did this perfectly. It was an easy matter for him to dress in the way I dressed. He was soon able to copy my movements and general manner. In spite of the weakness in his speech, he even copied my voice. He could not produce my louder sounds, of course, but the *key* – it was exactly mine. After a time his strange whisper became *the perfect model of my own voice*. The success of all this may be imagined when I say that we were the same size, and as alike in appearance as two brothers.

The only comfort that I could find in this situation was that no one else seemed to notice it. Wilson himself was the only one who laughed at me. Why the whole school did not sense his plan, notice it being put into action, and join in the laughter, was a question that I could not answer. Perhaps the success, the perfection of his copy, was what made it so difficult to recognize.

3

Wilson had another habit that made me very angry. He loved to give me advice. He gave it in a way that seemed to suggest that I badly needed it. I did not like this at all, and I refused to listen. But I must admit now that none of his suggestions were mistaken or unwise. His moral sense was far greater than my own. In fact, I might have been a better and a happier man if I had more often accepted him as my guide.

As it was, I grew more and more to dislike his unpleasant interruptions. But it was not until the end of my stay at the school that I really began to hate him. It was at about this time that I had a strange experience with him. We had had a more than usually violent quarrel, and because he had not expected to see me, he spoke and acted in an unusually open way. I discovered in his voice, his manner and his appearance something which first surprised me and then deeply interested me. I sensed that I had known him before – in some distant past, perhaps, or in some earlier life. The feeling (it was more a feeling than a thought) disappeared as quickly as it came; and I mention it now simply because it was the last time I spoke to him at school.

One night, just before I left the school, I decided to try to play one more joke on him. While everyone was sleeping, I got up and, carrying a lamp, went to Wilson's bedroom. I opened the curtains around his bed, and saw that he was sleeping. I looked – and as I looked a feeling of icy coldness flowed through my body. My legs and arms shook, the blood seemed to leave my head, and I felt sick with fear. Struggling for breath, I lowered the lamp to his face. Was *this* the face of William Wilson? I saw that it was, but I trembled at what I saw. He did not look like *this* – certainly not like this – when he was awake. The same name! The same appearance! The same day of arrival at the school! I thought of his determined and meaningless copying of my walk, my voice, my manner and my habits. Was it possible that Wilson's face, *as I saw it now*, was simply the result of his careful practice in copying of my own? Shaken and unable to think clearly, I put out the lamp and left the room. Before morning came I had left the school, and I never returned to it again.

A few months later I went to Eton.★ This change of scene caused me to forget the other school, and I thought no more about my namesake. I lived a very lazy and aimless life and hardly studied at all. I shall not describe those three wasted years, during which the roots of evil became firmly established. My story moves on to the end of that time. One evening, after a week of hard drinking, I invited a small group of my wildest friends to a secret party in my rooms. The wine flowed freely, but there were other, even more enjoyable and dangerous attractions. The first light of day could already be seen in the east, when the voice of a servant was heard outside the room. He said that some person, who seemed to be in a great hurry, wanted to speak to me in the hall.

As I stepped outside into the shadows, I saw the figure of a youth about my own size. He was dressed in a white coat just like my own. He rushed towards me, took me by the arm, and bent his head to mine; and then I heard the voice, the low *whisper*, 'William Wilson!', in my ear. He raised a finger and shook it violently, as a grave warning. This movement of his brought a thousand memories racing to my mind – they struck it with the shock of an electric current. And then in a moment he was gone.

For some weeks after this event I made many enquiries. I knew, of course, that my unwelcome visitor was my namesake. But who and what was this Wilson? – and where did he come from? – and what did he want with me? But I could find out nothing of importance about him. I learned only that he had left that other school, because of a sudden accident in his family, on the same day that I myself had gone.

★ *Eton*: a famous English private school.

5

A little later I went to Oxford to attend the University. Here the foolish generosity of my parents allowed me to continue a life of wasteful pleasure. And it was at Oxford that I learned the evil art of cheating; this shows how far I had fallen from the state of a gentleman. Actually, it was only the seriousness of this offence that allowed me to practise it. My friends, all of them, would rather have doubted the clearest proofs than have suspected me of such behaviour; for I was the happy, the generous William Wilson.

After I had successfully cheated at cards for years, a rich young man named Glendinning came to the University. He had a weak character and seemed the perfect person for my purpose. I often played with him, and managed to let him win one or two fairly large amounts of money from me. In this way he fell deeper into my trap. At last my plan was ready. I met him at the rooms of a friend who knew nothing about my cheating. There were eight or ten young men present. I carefully directed the conversation until it was Glendinning himself who suggested a game of cards. We played for a long time, and at last he and I sat alone at the table while the rest of the company stood around us looking on. In a very short time Glendinning, who was drinking heavily, owed me a lot of money. Less than an hour later his debt was four times as great. I did not believe, though, that such a loss could account for Glendinning's extreme paleness; for he now looked as white as death. His family, I had heard, was one of the wealthiest in England. I thought that the wine must be affecting him and I was about to suggest that we stopped the game, when I was surprised by some remarks from our friends and a cry of hopelessness from Glendinning. I understood then that I had ruined him completely and that he had everyone's sympathy for his miserable position.

There was silence in the room, and some of those present looked at me angrily. My face was burning, and I do not know

6

what I might have done, if we had not been suddenly interrupted. The door of the room burst open, and a violent wind blew out the lamps. Their light, as it died, showed us that a stranger had entered and was now standing among us. And then we heard his voice.

'Gentlemen,' he said, in a low, clear and never-to-be-forgotten *whisper*, which brought a lump to my throat, 'I am sorry for this interruption, but it is a duty. You do not know the true character of the person who has tonight won a large amount of money from Lord Glendinning. I advise you to examine the inside of his coat.' Then he left the room as quickly as he had entered. How can I describe my feelings? How can I explain that the *feeling* of guilt is a thousand times worse than the fact? But I had little time for thought. Many hands roughly seized me, and the lights were relit. A search followed. All the picture cards necessary for the game that we had played were found in a large pocket on the inside of my coat. Several sets of cards carefully arranged to give me a definite advantage were found in other inside pockets.

My friends received this discovery with silent disbelief, and their silence troubled me more than any burst of anger would have done.

'Mr Wilson,' said our host at last, 'we have had enough of your skill at cards. I hope you will leave Oxford. In any case, you will leave my rooms immediately.'

Early the next morning, experiencing the bitter pain of shame, I began a hurried journey to Paris.

But I could not escape. In Paris Wilson again interrupted my affairs. Years went by, and I still could not lose him. In Rome – at the height of my success – he stepped in again! In Vienna, too – and in Moscow! I ran again; he followed; to the ends of the earth I ran, but *could never be rid of him*.

Whenever Wilson involved himself in any action of mine, he did so with a single intention: to prevent some plan which might have caused serious harm. I gained no comfort from knowing this. I felt only anger over the loss of my natural freedom of action. He had continued, for very many years, to copy my dress. But I had not once since we were at school together seen his face. Whoever he was, whatever he was, the hiding of his face seemed to me the greatest foolishness. Surely he knew that I recognized him? He could not fail to understand that, to me, he was always the William Wilson of my schooldays – the hated namesake, companion, competitor. But let me hurry to the end of my story.

By this time I had become a heavy drinker; and the effect of wine on my temper caused me to lose all patience with my namesake. I was in Rome in the year 18—, and I decided to suffer no longer. One evening I attended a dance at the home of a rich man of good family. He was a gentleman of great age, who was married to a young, happy and beautiful wife. I had arranged to meet the lady in the garden; I will not tell you the shameful purpose of my plan. I was hurrying there when I felt a light hand on my shoulder, and heard that low, ever-remembered *whisper* in my ear.

I turned on him angrily and seized him by the collar. He was dressed, as I expected, exactly as I was, and we both wore swords. His face was entirely covered by a mask of black silk.

'Devil!' I shouted, 'you shall trouble me no longer! Show me your sword!'

He paused for a moment. Then, slowly, he prepared to defend himself.

It was soon over. I was wild with every kind of excitement. I felt that I could have fought an army. In a few seconds he was at my mercy, and I drove my sword repeatedly through his chest.

At that moment I thought I heard a footstep behind me. I looked around, but there was no one there. I then turned to my dying enemy. I cannot in ordinary language describe the terrible fear that filled me when I looked at him. He was very pale, and there was blood on his clothes. But in spite of these things, I could see that every mark and every line of his face, every thread of his dress, was in the smallest detail *my own*!

It was Wilson; but he no longer spoke in a whisper. I might have imagined that I myself was speaking while he said:

'*You have won, and I have lost. But, from now on you too are dead – dead to the World, to Heaven, and to Hope! You existed in me – and this body is your own. See how completely you have, through my death, murdered yourself.*'

The Gold-Bug

My friendship with Mr William Legrand began many years ago. He had once been wealthy, but a number of misfortunes had made him poor; and to avoid the shame of his situation, he had gone to live at Sullivan's Island, near Charleston, South Carolina.

He had built himself a small hut, and was living there with an old servant called Jupiter, when I first met him. He was an educated man and had unusual powers of mind which interested me greatly. His chief amusements were shooting and fishing, and he was a keen collector of shells and insects.

One cold afternoon, about the middle of October, 18—, I went to the island to visit my friend. On reaching the hut I knocked, as was my custom. Getting no reply, I looked for the key where I knew it was hidden, unlocked the door, and went in. I was glad to see that a fine fire was burning. I threw off my coat, and settled down by the fire to wait for my hosts.

They arrived as it was getting dark, and gave me the warmest of welcomes. Jupiter hurried to prepare a duck for supper, while Legrand began to describe a strange insect which he had found that afternoon, and which he believed to be of a completely new kind.

'If I had only known you were here!' said Legrand. 'I would have kept it to show you. But on the way home I met my friend G—, and very foolishly I lent him the insect. It is of a bright gold colour – about the size of a large nut – with two black spots near one end of the back, and another, a little longer, at the other. Jupiter here thinks the bug is solid gold and, improbable as it seems, I'm not sure that he is wrong.'

Here Jupiter interrupted with, 'That I do; I never felt half so heavy a bug in all my life.'

'Really,' said Legrand, 'you never saw gold that shone brighter than this little thing; but let me give you some idea of the shape.'

He sat down at a small table, on which were a pen and ink, but no paper. He looked for some in a drawer, but found none.

'Never mind,' he said, 'this will do.' And he took from his pocket a piece of what looked like dirty notepaper, on which he made a rough drawing with the pen. When he had finished, he brought the paper over to where I was still sitting by the fire, and gave it to me. While I was studying the drawing we were interrupted by the arrival of Legrand's dog, which jumped on my shoulders and covered me with affection; I was one of his favourite visitors. When he had finished, I looked at the paper and was confused by what my friend had drawn.

'Well!' I said, 'this is a strange insect. It looks like a skull to me.'

'A skull!' repeated Legrand. 'Oh – yes – well, it may look like that on paper. The two black spots look like eyes, I suppose, and the longer one at the bottom like a mouth.'

'Perhaps so,' I said, 'but, Legrand, you are a poor artist.'

'No,' he said, a little annoyed, 'I draw quite well; at least my teachers used to think so.'

'Well, my dear friend, you must be joking then,' I said. 'This is a very good skull, but a very poor insect.'

I could see that Legrand was becoming quite angry, so I handed him the paper without further remark. His bad temper surprised me – and, as for the drawing, it *did* look exactly like a skull.

He took the paper roughly, and was going to throw it into the fire when something about the drawing suddenly seemed to hold his attention. His face grew violently red – then as pale as death. For some minutes he continued to examine the paper, turning it in all directions, but saying nothing. At last he took from his coat pocket an envelope, placed the paper carefully in it, and locked both in the drawer of his desk.

This behaviour of Legrand was strange, and I was disappointed that, for the rest of the evening, he remained lost in thought. When

11

I rose to leave, he did not invite me to stay the night, as he usually did, but he shook my hand with more than ordinary feeling.

It was about a month after this (during which I had seen nothing of Legrand) that Jupiter visited me at Charleston. He brought bad news; his master was ill and in need of help. The sickness, according to Jupiter, was caused by a bite which Legrand had received from the gold-bug on the day when he had caught the insect. Jupiter himself, had escaped being bitten only through taking hold of the creature in a piece of paper. The old man then produced a letter from Legrand addressed to me.

> My dear —
>
> Why have I not seen you for so long a time? I hope you have not been foolish enough to take offence at anything I said last time we met. I have something to tell you, but I hardly know how to tell it, or whether I should tell it at all.
>
> I have not been well for some days, and poor old Jupiter annoys me with his attentions. I find the greatest difficulty in getting away from him in order to spend some time among the hills on the mainland.
>
> If it is convenient, come over with Jupiter. *Do* come. I wish to see you *tonight*, on business of importance, of the *highest* importance.
>
> Ever yours,
> WILLIAM LEGRAND.

This note caused me great anxiety. What business 'of the highest importance' could *he* possibly have to deal with? I feared that the continued weight of misfortune had at last brought him close to losing his mind. I decided immediately that I must go with the servant.

Jupiter, I noticed, was carrying three new spades, which, he said, Legrand had ordered him to buy in Charleston, though for

12

what purpose the old man had no idea at all. 'It's the bug, sir,' he said to me. 'All this nonsense comes from the bug.'

It was about three in the afternoon when we arrived at the hut. Legrand looked terribly pale and ill, and his dark eyes shone with a strange, unnatural light. At his first words, my heart sank with the weight of lead.

'Jupiter is quite right about the bug. It is of *real gold*, and it will make my fortune,' he said seriously.

'How will it do that?' I asked sadly.

He did not answer, but went to a glass case against the wall, and brought me the insect. It was very beautiful, and, at that time, unknown to scientists. It was very heavy, and certainly looked like gold, so that Jupiter's belief was quite reasonable; but I simply failed to understand Legrand's agreement with that opinion.

'My dear friend,' I cried, 'you are unwell, and –'

'You are mistaken,' he interrupted, 'I am as well as I can be under the excitement from which I am suffering. If you really wish me well, you will take away this excitement.'

'And how can I do this?'

'Very easily. Jupiter and I are going on a journey into the hills, and we shall need the help of some person whom we can trust. Whether we succeed or fail in our purpose, the weight of the excitement which I now feel will be removed.'

'I am anxious to help you in any way,' I replied; 'but I believe this business of the insect is complete nonsense. I want you to promise me, on your honour, that when this journey is over, you will return home and follow my advice, as if I were your doctor.'

'Yes; I promise,' said Legrand; 'and now let us go, for we have no time to lose.'

With a heavy heart I set out with my friend. We started at about four o'clock – Legrand, Jupiter, the dog and myself. Jupiter was carrying the three spades; I was in charge of two lamps; Legrand took only the goldbug, tied to the end of a long piece of

13

string, which he swung as he walked. Tears came to my eyes when I saw this last, clear proof of my friend's mental sickness.

Our path led across to the mainland, and on to the high ground to the north-west. We walked for about two hours, and the sun was just setting when we arrived at a natural platform towards the top of a hill, which was surrounded by forest and large rocks. The place was overgrown with bushes. Legrand went straight towards a great tree, which stood, with about eight or ten others, on the level ground. This tree was taller and more beautiful than any I have ever seen, and the wide spread of its branches threw shadows over its smaller neighbours. When we reached this tree, Legrand turned to Jupiter, and asked him if he thought he could climb it. The old man seemed surprised by the question, and for some moments made no reply. At last, after a careful examination of the tree, he simply said: 'Yes, I can climb it. How far up must I go, master?'

'Get up the main trunk first, and then I will tell you which way to go – and here – stop! Take the bug with you.'

'The gold-bug, master!' cried Jupiter, in some fear. 'Why must I take that?'

'Do as I tell you,' said Legrand, handing him the string to which the insect was still tied; 'now, up you go.'

The servant took hold of the string and began to climb. This part of the strange business was not difficult; the tree was old, and its trunk uneven, with a number of good footholds. Within a short time, the climber was sixty or seventy feet from the ground.

'Keep going up the main trunk,' shouted Legrand, 'on this side – until you reach the seventh branch.'

Soon Jupiter's voice was heard, saying that he could count six branches below the one on which he was sitting.

'Now, Jupiter,' cried Legrand, with much excitement, 'climb out along that branch as far as you can. Tell me if you see anything strange.'

14

When I heard these words, I decided, with great sorrow, that there could now be no doubt about the state of my friend's mind. I felt seriously anxious about getting him home. While I was wondering what was best to be done, Jupiter's voice was heard again.

'I'm getting along, master; soon be near the ... o-o-oh! God have mercy! What *is* this here?'

'Well!' cried Legrand, highly excited. 'What is it?'

'It's a skull,' said Jupiter, 'and it's fixed to the tree with a nail.'

'Well now, Jupiter, do exactly as I tell you – do you hear?'

'Yes, master.'

'Give me your attention, then – find the left eye of the skull, and let the bug drop through it, as far as the string will reach – but be careful and do not let go of the string.'

'The left eye, master? Yes, yes, I have it! It's a very easy thing to put the bug through this hole – can you see it there below?'

We could now see the insect at the end of the string, shining, like a little ball of gold, in the last light of the setting sun. Legrand immediately used one of the spades to beat back the bushes and clear a circular space, three or four yards across, just below the insect. He ordered Jupiter to let go of the string and come down from the tree.

My friend now pressed a small stick into the ground at the exact place where the insect fell. He took from his pocket a long tape measure, one end of which he fixed to the trunk of the tree at its nearest point to the stick. He then unrolled the tape, so that it touched the stick and continued outwards for a distance of fifty feet. Jupiter went in front of him, clearing away the bushes with a spade. At fifty feet a second stick was pressed into the ground; and around this the ground was again cleared in a rough circle about four feet across. Taking a spade himself, and giving one to Jupiter and one to me, Legrand begged us to begin digging as quickly as possible.

To tell the truth, I had no wish for further exercise. I would have refused if I could have done so without upsetting my poor friend. But he was now wildly excited, and I judged it wiser to take the spade with at least a show of being helpful.

By the light of the lamps we dug very steadily for two hours, and reached a depth of five feet without meeting anything of greater interest than soil and stones. Then we rested, and I began to hope that the nonsense was at an end. But Legrand, although clearly very disappointed, wiped his face thoughtfully and began again. We had dug out the whole circle, and now we dug deeper for another two feet. Still nothing appeared. At last my friend climbed up to the surface, with a look of bitter defeat on his face. He slowly put on his coat, which he had thrown off at the beginning of his work. Jupiter picked up the tools, and we turned in deep silence towards home.

We had taken a few steps in this direction, when, with a loud cry, Legrand seized Jupiter by the collar.

'You stupid fool!' he shouted. 'You good-for-nothing – answer me at once – which – which is your left eye?'

'Oh, my God, master! Isn't this my left eye?' cried the old man, placing his hand on his *right* eye, and holding it there as if afraid that his master might try to tear it out.

'I thought so! – I knew it! Hurrah!' cried Legrand. 'Come! We must go back.' Then, speaking more calmly, he said, 'Jupiter, was it this eye or that,' – here he touched each of the poor man's eyes – 'through which you dropped the bug?'

'It was this eye, master – the left eye – just as you told me,' – and here it was again his *right* eye that the servant touched.

'All right; that is enough; we must try it again.'

We returned to the tree. My friend moved the stick which marked the place where the insect had fallen to a place slightly west of its former position. He took the tape measure again from the tree to the stick, as before, and continued in a straight line to the distance of fifty feet. We now reached a point several yards away from the hole which we had dug. Around this new position another circle was marked, and we again set to work with the spades.

We had been digging in silence for, perhaps, an hour and a half, when we were interrupted by the violent crying of the dog. Suddenly he jumped into the hole, and began digging wildly. In a few seconds we saw human bones, the remains of two complete bodies. These were mixed with dust which appeared to be decayed clothing. One or two more spadefuls brought up the blade of a large knife. As we dug further, three or four loose pieces of gold and silver coin suddenly shone in the light of our lamps.

Legrand urged us to continue, and he had hardly spoken when a large ring of iron appeared; we soon found that this was part of a strong wooden box. We worked hard, and the ten minutes that followed were the most exciting in my life. The box was three and a half feet long, three feet wide, and two and a half feet deep. The ring was one of six – three on each side – by means of which six persons might have carried the box. But we could hardly move it. Luckily the lid was held shut by only two sliding bars. Breathless and trembling with anxiety, we pulled these back. A treasure of the greatest value lay shining before us. As the beams of our lamps fell on the box, the light from the pile of gold and jewels flashed upward and caused us to turn our eyes away in pain.

I shall not pretend to describe the feelings with which I looked on that wealth. We said nothing, and made no movement, I suppose, for two minutes. Then Jupiter, as if in a dream, fell down on his knees. He buried his arms up to his shoulders in gold, and said quietly: 'And all this comes from the gold-bug; all from the little gold-bug!'

It was necessary at last to think of moving the treasure before daylight. After a short discussion, we decided to lighten the box by taking out, and hiding in the bushes, more than half of the heavier pieces. Leaving the dog to guard them, we hurried away with the box. After an extremely tiring journey, we reached the hut in safety at one o'clock in the morning. We rested until two, and had supper; and then we returned to the hills with three strong bags. A little before four o'clock we arrived at the hole, where we divided the rest of the treasure, as equally as possible, among us. We reached the hut, for the second time, just as the faint light of day appeared over the treetops in the east.

After a further rest, we examined and sorted the treasure with great care. We soon found that we now possessed wealth far greater than we had originally imagined. In coins there was more than 450,000 dollars. There was not one piece of silver; it was all ancient gold of great variety – money from all the countries of Europe. The value of the jewels and the hundreds of golden plates and cups and rings was more difficult to judge. Their total weight of almost 400 English pounds did not include 197 beautiful gold watches, three of which were worth at least 500 dollars each. We calculated that the whole treasure was worth a million and a half dollars, but we later found that the actual value was far greater.

The following evening Legrand gave me a full account of what had led him to this discovery. 'You remember,' he said, 'the piece of paper on which I drew for you a picture of the insect.'

'The insect that looked like a skull?' I asked.

'Yes; well, the paper was, in fact, a piece of very fine animal skin. When you gave it back to me, I, too, saw a skull where I had drawn the bug. But a moment later I saw my drawing on the back of the skin. This was strange; I was sure that both sides of the skin, though dirty, had been unmarked when I made my drawing.

'That night, after you had gone, and when Jupiter was fast asleep, I tried to solve the mystery. I remembered that the piece of skin had been found half buried in the sand, near the place where we had caught the insect. Jupiter had picked it up, and used it to take hold of the creature, which he was afraid might bite him. I had wrapped the insect in the skin, and carried it like that until we met my friend G——. Then, after lending him the bug, I must have put the skin, without thinking, into my pocket.

'As I sat in deep thought, I remembered another strange fact. It was this: at the place where we had found the insect, I had noticed the ancient wreck of a boat – only a few pieces of wood remained – on the shore. So here was a sort of *connection* – a wrecked boat, and, near it, a piece of skin – *not paper* – with a skull drawn on it. You know, of course, that the skull is the usual sign of those who rob at sea – that a flag with the skull on it is raised as they attack.'

'But,' I interrupted, 'you say that the paper – or skin – was unmarked when you made your drawing of the insect. How, and when, then, did the skull appear?'

'Ah, that was the whole mystery; although it did not remain one for long. Every detail of the chain of events came back to my mind. On the evening of your visit the weather was cold (oh, lucky accident!), and you were sitting close to the fire. Just as I placed the skin in your hand, and as you were about to examine my drawing, the dog entered, and jumped on you. With one hand you played with him, while your other hand, holding the skin, must have fallen towards the fire. When at last you looked at the skin, you saw a skull drawn there; but my drawing of the insect was on *the other side* – the side which you did not look at. It seemed reasonable to me, when I thought about the matter that night, to suppose that the *heat* of the fire had brought out the drawing of the skull. It is well known that certain substances exist, by means of which it is possible to write on paper or skin, so that the letters can be seen only when the paper is heated. The writing disappears, sooner or later, when the material is removed from heat, but always reappears when it is heated.

'To test the strength of this idea I immediately built up the fire, and thoroughly heated the piece of skin. In a few minutes there appeared in the corner opposite to the skull the figure of a baby goat – *a kid*. Well, you must have heard of the famous *Captain Kidd*, and I immediately decided that the drawing of the animal must represent his signature. I say signature, because its position in the bottom right-hand corner of the piece of skin strongly suggested this idea. In the same way, the skull at the top appeared as a kind of official stamp.'

'But was there no message,' I asked, 'between the stamp and the signature?'

'Not at first; but my belief that some great good fortune lay near was so strong that I continued to examine the skin. Piling wood on the fire, I warmed some water, and carefully washed it. It was coated with dirt, and I thought that this might have something to do with the failure. While it was drying, I thought about Captain Kidd and the treasure that he is said to have buried somewhere along this coast. He was a daring and successful robber, and the stories of his hidden wealth would not have existed so long and so continuously without at least *some* truth in them. You will remember that the stories are all about searching for money, not about finding it; and this suggested to me that the gold remained buried. I thought that some accident – such as the loss of a note showing its position – might have prevented Kidd or the other robbers from finding it again. I now felt a hope, nearly amounting to certainty, that the piece of skin so strangely found contained a lost record of the place of burial.'

'What did you do next?'

'I placed the skin in a pan, with the figures of the skull and the kid face down, and put the pan on the burning wood. In a few minutes, I took off the pan, and examined the skin. To my great joy, the whole was just as you see it now.'

Here Legrand, having heated the skin again, as he was

speaking, handed it to me. In red print, between the skull and the goat, the following signs appeared:

```
53‡‡†305))6★28))‡.)—5);086★
;48†8§60))85;1‡(;:‡*8†83(88)*‡(;485);5*†2:
★‡(;4)8§8*;42(5*—485);)6†8
)4‡‡;I(‡9;4808I;8:8‡I;48†85;4)
485†506*8I(‡9;48;(88;4(‡?34;48
)4‡;I6I;:I88;‡;
```

'It is beyond my power,' I said, returning the skin to him, 'to understand what this means.'

'And yet,' said Legrand, 'the solution is not very difficult; for Kidd, as you might imagine, was not a very clever man. The figures and signs have a meaning; and a little practice with mysteries of this sort has made it easy for me to understand them. I have solved others a thousand times more difficult than this.

'The first question that one must usually ask is this: in what language is the message written? In this case it is no problem at all; for the drawing of a goat, or kid, in place of Kidd's real signature, makes it clear that the language used is English.

'The next step is to find the figure, or sign, that appears *most frequently* in the message. I saw at once that the figure 8 is the most common, but perhaps it is best to count them all if you are in doubt. Now, in English, the most common letter is *e*. Let us suppose, then, that the figure 8 stands for the letter *e*. Let us see next if the 8 often appears in pairs – for the *e* is very often doubled in English, in such words, for example as "meet", "speed", "seen", "been", "agree", etc. We find that the 8 is doubled three times in this short message. We may now feel quite sure that the figure 8 represents *e*.

'Of all the *words* in the English language, the most common is "the". We should now look at the message to see if we can find any groups of three characters, in the same order each time, the last character being 8. We see immediately that the group ;48 is repeated, in that order, not less than five times. We may believe, then, that ;48 represents the word "the". We now know that ; represents *t* and that the figure 4 stands for *h*.

'Look next at the last but one appearance of the group ;48 towards the end of the message. We may write the known letters, like this:

    ;48;(88;4
    thet.eeth

'We have here the word "the", followed by parts of two other words. I say two, because there is no single word of six letters in English that begins with *t* and ends with *eeth*. By trying all the possible letters, we find that the missing letter must be *r*, giving us the word "tree". The sign (, then, represents the letter *r*.

'The group ;48 helps us again if we examine its last use in the message. We see this arrangement:

    ;48;(88;4(‡?34;48
    thetreethr...hthe

'The missing letters are, quite clearly, *oug*, giving us the word "through", and we now have three more letters, *o*, *u*, and *g*, represented by ‡, ?, and 3.

'I continued in this way to find the other letters, making full use of those already known to me. I wrote down, for example, the group 83(88, which is not far from the beginning of the note:

    †83(88
    .egree

'This can only be the word "degree", giving me the letter *d*, represented by the sign †.

'It is hardly necessary, I think, for me to go on with the details of the solution. I have said enough to give you an idea of *how* a solution is reached, and to show you that it was not particularly difficult to translate into words. But I did have to make use of my knowledge of this area. Here is my translation:

> A good glass in Bessop's Castle in the devil's seat − forty-one degrees − north-east and by north − seventh branch east side − shoot from the left eye of the death's head − a line from the tree through the shot fifty feet out.

'I had heard of a family named Bessop, who were great landowners, at one time, in this part of the country. I made careful enquiries among the older people of the place, and at last met a woman of great age who had been in service with the family very many years ago. She had heard of a place called Bessop's Castle, and thought that she could guide me to it, but said that it was not a castle at all, but a high rock.

'We found it without much difficulty. It was an irregular group of rocks − one of the rocks being far higher than the others and quite like the tower of a castle in its general shape. I climbed to the top of this tower, and sat there wondering what should be done next.

'Suddenly my eyes fell on a narrow shelf of rock, about a yard below where I sat. It was shaped exactly like a chair with a back and a seat, and I had no doubt that here was the "devil's seat" mentioned in the note. I lowered myself to it, and found that it was impossible to sit on it except in one particular position. Now I understood the meaning of the message.

'The "good glass" did not mean a drinking glass at all, but a seaman's glass − or telescope − to be used from the only possible

23

sitting position in the "devil's seat". And the words "forty-one degrees – north-east and by north" were directions for pointing the glass. Greatly excited, I hurried home, found my telescope, and returned to the rock.

'Judging the direction as best I could by my watch and the position of the sun, I moved the telescope slowly up and down. My attention was drawn to a circular opening in the leaves at the top of a great tree in the distance. In the centre of this opening, I saw a white spot, which, in a moment or two, I recognized as a human skull.

'All was now clear to me. The skull was to be found on the seventh branch on the east side of that particular tree. I had to "shoot", or drop something, from the left eye of the skull to the ground; and then to mark a line from the tree, through the place where "the shot" fell, and outwards to a distance of fifty feet. Beneath that point, I thought it *possible* that a treasure lay hidden.

'The next day, with some difficulty, I found the tree and sent for you; and you know the rest of the adventure as well as I do myself.'

'I suppose,' I said, 'that you missed the treasure, in the first attempt at digging, through Jupiter's stupidity in letting the bug fall through the right eye instead of through the left.'

'Exactly. That mistake made a difference of five or six yards in the position of the gold.'

'Yes, I see; and now there is only one thing that I don't understand. How do you explain the bones found in the hole?'

'There seems only one way of explaining them – though it is terrible to believe in such cruelty. Kidd must have had help in burying the treasure. Then, when the work was finished, perhaps he thought it better that no one should share the secret with him. Two shots, while his men were busy in the hole, may have been enough; or perhaps it required more – who can tell?'

The Fall of the House of Usher

During the whole of a dull, dark and silent day in the autumn of the year, I had travelled alone, on horseback, towards the House of Usher. As I came in sight of the place, my spirits sank; they grew as dark and dull as the sky above me, and as sad as the cold, grey walls of the building before my eyes. I did not know the reason for this feeling of extreme misery, unless it resulted from the general appearance of decay about the house, and about the grounds which surrounded it. There were the great dark windows, like black eyes in an empty face. The white trunks of lifeless trees stood out on the banks of a lake, whose still waters acted as a mirror to the scene above. The scene mirrored in the lake seemed even more sorrowful than the reality. In the end I gave up my attempts to solve the mystery of my anxiety. I left the lake, and went on to the house.

The owner of the property, Roderick Usher, had been one of the closest of my childhood friends, but some years had passed since our last meeting. He had recently sent me a very urgent invitation to visit him – had begged me, in fact, to stay with him for several weeks. He wrote that he was suffering from a severe illness, a mental disorder. My companionship, he thought, would cheer him, and bring calm to his troubled thoughts. He was so sincere about all this, and much more, that I did not think twice; and here I was, at the House of Usher.

Although, as boys, we had been the best of friends, I really knew little about Roderick Usher. I remembered that he had always been very quiet, and liked to keep himself apart from other people. His ancient family had been noted, through the centuries, for their sensitivity and imagination; and these had shown themselves in many great works of art and music. I knew, too, the very unusual fact that there were no branches to the family of Usher. The name and possessions had simply passed, without any interruption, from father to son. 'The House of Usher' meant, to the people of the area, not only the property but also the family.

As I came near the great grey building, a strange idea took shape in my mind. I sensed that the air which surrounded the house was different from the rest of God's air. I felt that it came from the decayed trees, and the grey walls, and the silent lake – that the air itself was grey. It hung about the place like a cloud. I had some difficulty in throwing off this foolish thought.

The house, now that I could see it clearly, looked extremely old. The building was still complete – I mean that no part of the stonework had fallen – but each separate stone was itself a powdery ruin of what it had once been. There were no other signs of weakness, except a long, narrow crack which ran from the roof right down the front of the house to the level of the ground.

A servant took my horse, and I entered the hall. I was then led, in silence, through many dark and narrow passages to the master's room. Much that I noticed on the way had a strange effect on me, although I had been used all my life to surroundings such as these – the expensive furniture, the heavy curtains, the weapons and the rows of pictures on the walls. On one of the stairways, I met the family doctor, who seemed both confused and frightened by my presence.

The room of my host, which I reached at last, was very large, high and dark, with a great deal of fine old furniture in it. Books and musical instruments lay scattered around, but somehow failed to give any life to the scene. I felt that I breathed an air of sorrow.

Usher greeted me warmly. We sat down, and for some moments I looked at him with a feeling of great pity. Surely, no man had ever before changed so terribly, and in so short a time! He had always been pale – but never as pale as this. His eyes, always attractive, were now unnaturally large and bright; his thin lips had been reduced to a line on his face; the fine, soft hair now floated, uncut, like that of an old man, around his face and neck.

The changed manner of my friend was equally striking. He was, all the time, in a state of high excitement or of great anxiety. As he passed quickly from one to the other of these conditions, his voice changed: the wild, high note would drop suddenly to a steady, careful sound, like the speech of a man who has drunk too much.

It was in this way that he spoke of my visit, of his great desire to see me, and of the comfort that he expected me to bring him. He began a long description of his disease. It was, he said, a family evil, for which there seemed to be no cure – a simple nervous disorder, he added, which would doubtless soon pass. He suffered a great deal from a sharpness of the senses. He could eat only tasteless food, and wear only a certain kind of clothing. He could not bear the smell of flowers. The faintest light brought pain to his eyes; and he had forbidden all sounds in the house, except those from certain musical instruments.

'I am afraid of the future,' he said; 'not the events of the future, but their effect on me. I tremble at the thought of any, even the smallest, event which may increase my anxiety. I am not afraid of danger, except its most extreme effect – terror. In my weakened state I feel that the time will sooner or later arrive when I must give up life and reason together, in my personal struggle with *Fear*.'

It was a great shock to me to learn that he had not left the house for many years. 'The house,' he said, '– the actual walls and towers of the building – have gained an influence over me, a strange power that holds me to them, as if they were living creatures.' I did not know what answer to make to my friend.

He admitted that much of the unhappiness which he suffered had a simple, and quite natural, origin. It was the long and severe illness of a greatly loved sister – his close companion for many years – his last and only relative on earth. 'She will die very soon,' he said, with a bitterness which I can never forget, 'and her death will leave me the last of the ancient family of Usher.' While he spoke, Lady Madeline (for that was her name) passed slowly through the room at the far end, and, without having noticed my presence, disappeared. I watched her with a surprise and deep fear that I could not account for. As soon as she had gone, I turned to my friend. He had covered his face with his hands to hide a flood of tears.

The disease of Lady Madeline had defeated the skill of her doctors, and she no longer cared whether she lived or died. A gradual but continuous loss of flesh caused a weakness of the body, which was made worse by the frequent stopping of the action of her heart. With great sorrow, my friend told me that there was little difference between these attacks and actual death. 'She will now have to remain in bed,' he said, 'and I do not think that you will see her alive again.'

For several days following my arrival at the house, neither of us mentioned her name. During this time I made great efforts to comfort and cheer my friend. We painted and read together; or I listened, as if in a dream, to the music which he played. We grew closer and closer in friendship, and shared our most secret thoughts. But it was all useless. Darkness continued to pour from his mind onto everything around us, in one endless flood of misery.

I shall always remember the many sad hours I spent like this alone with the master of the House of Usher. But I cannot properly explain our studies and activities in words. He was a man of high beliefs which had become confused during his long illness. He could now express these beliefs and feelings only in colours and sound – in the wildest kind of painting, and in difficult music that he wrote himself. The results were not clear even to himself. It may be imagined how hard it was for me to understand them!

I thought that in one of his pictures the idea was a little clearer, although I myself could not understand it. I have remembered that picture because it caused me to tremble as I looked at it. It showed a very long passage, with low walls, smooth and white. The background suggested that the passage was very far below the surface of the earth, but there was no way out of it that I could see. No lamps were shown, nor any other artifical light; but the whole scene was bathed in a flood of bright light.

During one of our discussions, Usher told me that he believed all plants had the power of feeling. He also thought that even lifeless objects would have this power under certain conditions. As I have already mentioned, this belief was connected with the grey stones of his home. He thought that the way they were arranged in the walls, and had been arranged for hundreds of years, gave them a life of their own. The waters of the lake, too, and the dead trees, shared this life, he said. 'The proof,' he added, ' – the proof off *feeling* in the walls and in the water – can be seen in the gradual but certain development of an air of their own about them.' I remembered my thoughts as I had come near the house, and I caught my breath. 'This air has had a silent and terrible influence on my family,' he said, 'and it has made *me* what I am.'

One evening Usher informed me, in a few words, that Lady Madeline was dead. It was his intention, he said, to keep her body for two weeks, before burial, in one of the many rooms below the house. His reason for this decision was not unnatural, as he had taken into account the particular kind of disease from which she suffered. In plain words, he wished to be sure that she was really dead before he placed her body in the family grave.

At the request of Usher, I helped him in making these arrangements. We two alone carried the body, in its box, to a small, dark room that lay below the part of the building where I myself slept. It had been used, in the troubled times of long ago, as a storeroom for gunpowder, or some other dangerous substance. Part of its floor, and the whole of a long passage through which we reached it, were lined with a red metal. The heavy iron door was protected in the same way. Having placed the box containing the body on a low table, we partly raised its lid and looked at the face inside. I immediately saw that brother and sister were exactly alike. Usher, guessing my thoughts, said that they had been twins, and that deep sympathies had always existed between them. There was a slight colour about her face and neck, and a faint smile – so terrible in death – on her lips. We did not look at her for long, but put back and nailed the lid, closed the iron door, and made our way back to the upper part of the house.

It was after three or four days of bitter grief that I noticed a change in the manner of my friend. His ordinary activities – his music, books and painting – were forgotten. He wandered from room to room, doing nothing, interested in nothing. He grew paler than ever and the brightness left his eye. There were times when I thought that he had a secret to tell me, and that he lacked the courage to tell it. At other times he sat for hours, listening with great attention to some imaginary sound, as if expecting something unusual to happen. Is it any wonder that his condition filled *me* with fear – that I felt the wild influences of his own strange but impressive beliefs spreading to *me*?

On the seventh or eighth night after the death of Lady Madeline, I experienced the full power of these feelings. For hours I lay awake, struggling against a sense of fear. I blamed my surroundings – the dusty furniture, the torn curtains which moved about in the wind of a rising storm, the ancient bed on which I lay. But my efforts were useless. At last, thoroughly afraid, I got up and looked as hard as I could into the darkness of the room. I heard – or thought that I heard – certain low sounds that came, from time to time, through the pauses in the storm. I dressed quickly, since I was trembling; but whether with cold or fear, I do not know. To calm myself I walked quickly backwards and forwards across the room.

I had done this two or three times when there was a gentle knock at my door and Usher entered, carrying a lamp. There was a look of crazy excitement in his eyes.

'And you have not seen it?' he cried suddenly. 'You have not – but, wait! You shall.' Saying this, and carefully shading his lamp, he hurried to one of the windows, and threw it open to the storm.

The force of the wind that entered nearly lifted us from our feet. But it was not the wind that held our attention, nor the thick clouds that flew in all directions about the house. We had no view of the moon or stars. But the building, and all the objects around us – even the clouds above – were shining in a strange, unnatural light. This light *poured* from the walls and from the waters of the lake.

'You must not – you shall not look at this!' I said, as I led him from the window to a seat. 'This light, which troubles you, is just an electrical disturbance of the air and not uncommon. Let us close the window; the wind is cold and dangerous to your health. Here is one of your favourite books. I will read, and you shall listen; and so we shall pass this terrible night together.'

I began to read, and Usher listened, or appeared to listen, with great attention. It was a well-known story by Sir Launcelot Canning. After I had been reading for eight or ten minutes, I reached the part where the chief character forces his way into the home of his enemy. At this point the story goes on as follows:

'And Ethelred lifted his sword, and struck the door with heavy blows. He cracked, and broke, and tore it apart, so that the noise of the dry and hollow-sounding wood seemed to fill the forest.'

At the end of this sentence I paused. I thought that I could hear, though faintly, just such a noise, like breaking wood. It seemed to come from some distant part of the house. It must have been, I believed, some damage caused by the storm; and I decided immediately that there was nothing in it to interest or worry me. I continued the story:

'Then the good Ethelred, entering through the door, was surprised to find a terrible creature standing guard in front of a palace of gold, with a floor of silver; and on the wall hung a great shining shield. There, on the shield, these words were written:

'He who enters here, has won a victory;

He who kills the guard, shall win the shield.'

'And Ethelred lifted his sword again, and struck the head of the creature, which died with cries so wild and terrible that they shook the walls. The metal shield then crashed to the floor at Ethelred's feet.'

Here again I felt afraid, and was forced to stop my reading. There was now no doubt at all that I *did* actually hear a faint, but clear cry of pain. It was closely followed by the distant sounds of metal being struck. I was not sure that Usher had himself heard these sounds, and I rushed, trembling, to the chair in which he sat. His eyes were fixed on the door; his lips were moving; and, as I bent over him, I heard the words.

'Do I hear it? – Yes, I hear it, and *have* heard it. Long – long long – for many minutes, many hours, many days, I have heard it – but I dared not – oh, pity me, miserable creature that I am! – I *dared* not speak! *We have put her living in that box*! Did I not tell you that my senses were sharp? I *now* tell you that I heard her first movements many days ago – but *I dared not speak*. And now – tonight – Ethelred – ha! ha! – the breaking of the door, and the death cry of the creature, and the crashing of the shield! – Say, instead, the forcing of the box, and her cries and struggles in the metal passage of her prison! Oh where shall I hide? Will she not soon be here? Is she not hurrying to punish me for my speed in burying her? Have I not heard her footstep on the stair? Can I not feel the heavy beating of her heart? Crazy fool!' – here he jumped to his feet, and shouted the words – 'CRAZY FOOL! I TELL YOU THAT SHE NOW STANDS OUTSIDE THE DOOR!'

As if in the force of his voice there was some special power, the great door opened. It was the work of the rushing wind – but then, outside the door, there did stand the tall, white clothed figure of Lady Madeline of Usher, covered in blood from some terrible struggle. For a moment she remained trembling in the doorway; then, with a low cry, she fell heavily inward onto her brother. The shock brought death to Usher immediately, and a moment later his sister died beside him.

I ran from that room and from that house in fear; and I did not look back until I had passed the lake. A great noise filled the air. As I watched, the crack – the crack that I have spoken of, that ran from the roof of the building to the ground – widened like the jaws of some terrible creature. The great walls broke apart. There was a sound like the voice of a thousand waters, and then the deep, dark lake closed over the ruins of the House of Usher.

The Red Death

The Red Death had killed thousands of people. No disease had ever been so terrible. There were sharp pains, and sudden fainting, and heavy bleeding through the skin; death came in half an hour. Red marks on the body, and especially on the face, separated the sufferer from all help and sympathy; and as soon as these signs appeared, all hope was lost.

But Prince Prospero was happy and brave and wise. When half his people had died, he called together a thousand of his lords and ladies, all cheerful and in good health, and with these he went to live in his most distant castle. The immense building, and its lands, were surrounded by a strong, high wall. This wall had gates of iron. The lords and their families, having entered, heated and melted the locks of the gates, and made sure that no key would ever open them again. The castle, which no one could now enter or leave, was well provided with food, and safe from the danger of disease. The world outside could take care of itself. Inside, it was foolish to worry, or to think. The prince had planned a life of pleasure. There were actors and musicians, there were beautiful things, there was wine. All these and safety were inside. Outside was the Red Death.

The court had been perhaps five or six months at the castle, and the disease had reached its height beyond the walls, when Prince Prospero entertained his thousand friends at an unusually grand masked dance.

Seven of the best rooms at the castle were specially arranged for the dance. These rooms were irregularly placed in one corner of the building, with sharp turns between them; so that it was hardly possible to see into more than one at a time. Each of the rooms was painted and decorated in a different colour, and the windows were of coloured glass to match the rooms. The room at the eastern end was coloured in blue – and its windows were bright blue. The second room was purple, and here the glass was purple. The third was all in green, the fourth in yellow, the fifth in orange, and the sixth in white. The seventh room was completely black, but its windows were different. They were the only ones that did not match the colour of the room. The glass here was a deep red – the colour of blood.

Now there were no lamps or lights inside any of these rooms. But *outside* each of the coloured windows, fires had been lit, and the flames produced strange and beautiful patterns in the rooms. In the black room, though, the effect of the firelight that shone through the red glass was terrible in the extreme. Few of the company were brave enough to enter this room.

In this seventh room, too, a great clock of black wood stood against the western wall. Whenever the time came for this clock to strike the hour, it produced a sound which was clear and loud and deep and very musical, but of such a strange note that the musicians stopped their playing to listen to it. So the dancing was interrupted, and there were a few moments of confusion among the happy company. Then, when the last stroke had ended, a light laughter broke out. The musicians looked at each other and smiled at their own foolishness, saying that they would certainly not allow the striking of the clock to interrupt their music at the next hour. But sixty minutes later there would be another pause, and the same discomfort and confusion as before.

In spite of these things, it was a cheerful party. There was beauty and originality in the dresses of the ladies, and much that was bright and imaginative in the clothing of the lords, although there were some who appeared frightening. The masked dancers moved between the seven rooms like figures in a dream. They moved in time to the music and changed colour as they passed from one room into the next. It was noticeable that, as the evening passed, fewer and fewer went near the seventh room – the black room, with its blood-red windows.

At last the great clock in this room began to strike the hour of midnight. And then the music stopped, as I have said, and the dancers stood still, and there was a feeling of discomfort among them all. Before the last of the twelve strokes had sounded, several of the more thoughtful dancers had noticed in the crowd a masked figure whom no one had seen before. His appearance caused first a whisper of surprise, that grew quickly into cries of fear, of annoyance, of terror.

The figure was tall and thin, and dressed from head to foot in the wrappings of the grave. The mask which covered his face was made to look so like that of a skull, that even the closest examination might not easily have proved it false. But the company present did not really object to any of this. Their annoyance and fear came from the fact that the stranger was dressed as the Red Death. His clothes were spotted with *blood* – and across his whole face were the *red marks* of death.

When the eyes of Prince Prospero fell on this terrible figure (which walked slowly among the dancers) his face reddened with anger.

'Who dares,' he demanded loudly of the lords and ladies who stood near him, 'who dares insult us in this way? Seize him and tear off the mask – so that we may know whom we have to hang at sunrise!'

The prince was standing in the eastern or blue room, as he said these words, with a group of his particular friends by his side. At first there was a slight movement of this group towards the strange figure, who, at the moment, was also near; but no one would put out a hand to seize him. He walked, without anyone stopping him, past the prince, through the blue room to the purple – through the purple to the green – through the green to the yellow – through this again to the orange – and even from there into the white room, before any firm movement was made to stop him. Then Prince Prospero, angry and ashamed at his own fear, rushed hurriedly through the six rooms, pulling out his sword as he went. The figure had reached the western wall of the seventh, the black room, when he turned suddenly towards the prince. There was a sharp cry and the sword fell to the floor. Immediately afterwards Prince Prospero fell dead.

Then, with a courage brought on by a sense of hopelessness, a crowd of the lords threw themselves on the stranger, who stood silent and still in the shadow of the great black clock. They tore at the mask of death and the bloody clothing – then stepped back, trembling with fear. There was no human form or body to be seen. The mask and the clothes were empty.

And now they knew that they were in the presence of the Red Death. He had come like a thief in the night. And one by one the dancers dropped and died in those halls of pleasure. The black clock struck once, and stopped. And the flames of the fires died out. And Darkness and Decay and the Red Death ruled over all.

The Barrel of Amontillado

I had suffered, as best I could, the thousand wrongs that Fortunato had done to me, but when he turned to insults, I swore that I would get revenge. I did not, of course, let any threat pass my lips. I waited for my chance patiently. I wanted to avoid the risk of failure; and if revenge is to succeed, two conditions are necessary. The wrongdoer must know that he is being punished, and by whom; and it must be impossible for him to hit back.

I continued to treat Fortunato kindly and to smile in his face. He did not realize that my smile was at the thought of his death.

Fortunato had one weakness, although he was, on the whole, a man to be respected and even feared. He was very proud of his knowledge of wine. On other subjects, he just pretended to be wise, but in the matter of wine he was sincere. We shared this interest. I knew a great deal about Italian wines myself, and bought large amounts whenever I could.

My chance came one evening during the holiday season. We met in the street. He had been drinking heavily, and he greeted me very warmly. He was dressed for the traditional celebrations, in a striped suit and a tall, pointed hat with bells. I was so pleased to see him that I thought I should never finish shaking his hand.

I said, 'My dear Fortunato, how lucky I am to meet you today. I have received a barrel of what claims to be Amontillado,★ but I have my doubts.'

'Amontillado?' he said. 'A barrel? Impossible! And in the middle of the celebrations!'

'I have my doubts,' I replied; 'and I was foolish enough to pay the full Amontillado price without asking you for advice. I could not find you, and I was afraid of losing it.'

'Amontillado!'

★ *Amontillado*: an expensive Spanish wine.

'I have my doubts, and I would like to be sure.'

'Amontillado!'

'As you are busy, I am on my way to Luchesi. He will be able to tell me ...'

'Luchesi cannot tell Amontillado from any other kind of wine.'

'But some fools say that his taste is a match for your own.'

'Come, let us go to your wine store.'

'My friend, no. Perhaps you have nothing to do, but I see that you have a very bad cold. My wine store is far below the ground, and it is very cold and wet there.'

'Let us go, anyway. The cold is nothing. Amontillado! You have been deceived. And as for Luchesi, he cannot tell a Spanish from an Italian wine.'

Fortunato took my arm. I put on a mask of black silk, and, turning up the high collar of my coat, I allowed him to hurry me to my house.

My servants were not at home. I had told them that I would not return until the morning, and had given them strict orders not to leave the house. I knew that these orders were enough to make them all disappear as soon as my back was turned.

I took two lamps from their stands, and, giving one to Fortunato, led him through to a long, narrow staircase. At the foot of this, deep underground, was the place where all the members of the Montresor family were buried. And there too, among the graves, was the family wine store.

My friend's walk was unsteady, and the bells on his cap rang as he moved.

'The barrel?' he said; and started coughing suddenly.

'It is further on,' I said. 'How long have you had that cough?'

My poor friend was unable to answer me for several minutes. 'It is nothing,' he said, at last.

'Come,' I said firmly, 'we will go back. Your health is

important. You are rich, respected, admired, loved; you are happy, as I was once. You will be ill, and I cannot be responsible. We will go back. There is always Luchesi ...'

'Enough,' he said, 'the cough is nothing. It will not kill me. I shall not die of a cough.'

'True – true,' I replied. 'I did not wish to frighten you – but you should take care. Here, a drink of this will help keep the cold out.'

I opened a bottle of fine old wine which I took from a long row that lay on the floor.

'Drink,' I said, handing him the wine.

He raised it to his lips with a smile. 'I drink,' he said, 'to the dead that lie around us.'

'And I to your long life.'

He took my arm again, and we went on.

'This place,' he said, 'is very large.'

'The Montresors,' I replied, 'were a great family, and large in number.'

The wine made his eyes shine, and the bells on his hat ring. We had passed between long walls of piled-up bones – the ancient remains of my family. We passed row after row of bottles and barrels.

'The air feels wetter here,' I said. 'We are below the river bed.'

I opened another bottle of wine and handed it to him. He emptied it almost at once. His eyes flashed. He laughed and threw the bottle over his shoulder.

'Let us see the Amontillado,' he said.

'Yes, the Amontillado,' I replied.

We went on down some steep steps, and finally reached a deep cave. Here the air was so bad that our lamps gave far less light than before. At the end of this cave, another smaller one appeared. Its walls had been piled to the roof with human remains, as the custom was many years ago. Three sides of this further cave were still decorated in this way. The bones had been thrown down from the fourth side, and lay in a pile on the floor. This wall showed another opening, about four feet deep and three wide, six or seven in height, which had been cut into the solid rock. The faint light from our lamps did not allow us to see into this small space.

'Go in,' I said; 'the Amontillado is in here. As for Luchesi —'

'He is a fool,' interrupted my friend, as he stepped unsteadily forward and climbed in, while I followed close behind. In a moment he had reached the far wall, and found his progress stopped by the rock. He stood still, confused, and wondering what to do. A moment later I had chained him to the rock. In its surface were two iron rings about two feet apart. A short chain hung from one of these, and a lock from the other. Throwing the chain around his waist, I turned the key in the lock in a few seconds. He was too surprised to react. Taking out the key, I stepped back to the entrance.

'Feel the wall,' I said. 'It is really very wet. Once more let me *beg* you to return. No? Then I must leave you. But I must first do all I can to keep out the cold air from your little room.'

'The Amontillado!' cried my friend in his confusion.

'Yes,' I replied; 'the Amiontillado.'

I walked across to the pile of bones in the middle of the floor. Throwing them to one side, I uncovered a quantity of building stone and some tools. With these I began to build a wall across the entrance to the little space.

I had laid the first row of stones, and had started the second, when a low cry came from inside; and this was followed by a wild shaking of the chain. The noise lasted for several minutes. I stopped work, and sat down on the stones in order to listen to it with more satisfaction. When at last the chain became silent, I continued my work, completing the second, third, fourth, fifth, sixth and seventh rows of stones, without interruption. The wall was now up to the level of my chest. I paused again, and held my lamp over the stonework, letting its weak beam fall on the figure inside.

Violent cries burst suddenly from the throat of the chained figure. They seemed to force me back from the wall. For a moment I stopped, I trembled; but I remained firm. I went on with my work. I shouted back at him. I repeated every sound he made – but louder. I did this, and at last he grew quiet.

It was now midnight, and I had reached the eleventh row – the last row – of stones. In a few minutes only a single stone remained to be fitted in. I struggled with its weight. I placed it partly in position. But now there came from inside a low laugh that made the hairs stand on my head. It was followed by a sad voice, which I could hardly recognize as that of Fortunato. The voice said: 'Ha! ha! ha! – a very good joke – an excellent joke. We shall have a good laugh about it – he! he! he! – over our wine!'

'The Amontillado!' I said.

'Ha! ha! ha! – yes, the Amontillado. But is it not getting late? They will be waiting for us – Lady Fortunato and the rest. Let us go.'

'Yes,' I said, 'let us go.'

'*For the love of God, Montresor!*'

'Yes,' I said, 'for the love of God!'

There was no reply to this. I called and called again; and at last I heard a ringing of the bells on his hat. My heart grew sick; it was the bad air down there that was affecting me, of course. I forced the last stone into position. I piled the bones up again, against the new wall. For half a century no one has moved them. Rest in peace!

The Whirlpool

We had reached the top of the highest rock, and now stood about fifteen or sixteen hundred feet above the angry seas that beat against the sharp, black edge of Lofoden. The old man was so out of breath that for some minutes he could not speak.

'Not long ago,' he said at last, 'I could have guided you here as well as the youngest of my sons; but not now. Now I feel broken in body and soul. Three years ago I suffered a terrible experience – such as no other human being has lived to describe. I passed through six hours of the worst fear that you can imagine; and in that time I grew old. In less than a day my hair changed from black to white, my arms and legs became weak, and my nerves were destroyed. I have brought you here so that you can have the best possible view of the scene of my suffering – and to tell you the whole story as you look at it.

'We are now,' my guide continued, 'very near the coast of Norway, and this rock that we are on is called Helseggen, the Cloudy. Sit down, lean forward very carefully, and look out onto the sea.'

A wide stretch of dark, almost black, ocean lay below us. To the right and left, as far as the eye could reach, stood lines of sharp-pointed rocks. A narrow band of white water marked the point where these rocks left the land and entered the sea. About five miles out to sea there was a small island with little growing on it. About two miles nearer the land, there was another, smaller one, surrounded by a ring of dark rocks. The appearance of the ocean, in the space between the more distant island and the shore, had something very unusual about it – the water was moving angrily in every direction, both with and against the wind.

'The further island,' went on the old man, 'is called Vurrgh. The nearer one is Moskoe. Do you hear anything? Do you see any change in the water?'

As the old man spoke, I noticed a loud and gradually increasing sound, like the noise of a heavy wind. At the same moment I saw that the movement of the sea below us was rapidly changing into a current that ran to the east. Even while I looked, the speed of this current increased almost beyond belief. Within five minutes the whole sea as far as Vurrgh was moving violently; but it was between Moskoe and the coast that the main disturbance lay. Here the wild waters, lifting, racing, thundering, turned and twisted in a thousand circles, and then rushed on to the east with frightening speed.

But in a few minutes the scene changed again. The surface grew smoother, and the whirlpools, spreading out to a great distance, combined to give birth to another, much larger one. Suddenly – very suddenly – this could be clearly seen in an immense circle more than a mile across. The edge of the whirlpool was represented by a broad belt of white water. The centre itself, as far as it was possible to see, was a smooth, shining, ink-black wall of water, sloping at about forty-five degrees to the horizon. Round and round it flew, sending out to the winds a frightening voice, half cry, half thunder, like nothing ever heard on earth.

The rock on which we were sitting trembled to its base. I threw myself flat on my face, and held tightly to the stone.

'This,' I said at last to the old man 'this *can* be nothing else than the great whirlpool of the Maelström.'

'So it is sometimes called,' he said. 'We Norwegians call it the Moskoe-ström, from the island of Moskoe.'

The written accounts of this whirlpool had certainly not prepared me for what I saw. The description given by Jonas Ramus, which is perhaps the best, does not in any way equal the reality; but perhaps he did not watch the scene from the top of Helseggen or during a storm. Some of the details that Ramus gives are interesting, although they are hardly powerful enough to give a clear idea of this natural wonder.

'When the tide is coming in,' Ramus says, 'the current runs rapidly up the coast between Lofoden and Moskoe. When it is going out, the sound is not equalled even by the loudest and most terrible waterfalls. The noise can be heard several miles away. The whirlpool is of such a width and depth that if a ship comes too near, it is pulled into the circle and carried down to the bottom, where it is beaten to pieces against the rocks. Then, when the tide begins to go out, the broken parts are thrown up again. The length of time between the tides, when the sea is more or less calm, is rarely more than a quarter of an hour, after which the violence gradually returns.'

This attempt of Jonas Ramus to explain the whirlpool as an action of the tides seemed reasonable enough to me when I first read it. But now, with the thunder in my ears, it seemed quite unsatisfactory. As I looked on the scene, my imagination found, for a moment, the belief of Kircher and others more acceptable. They thought that there must be a hole or crack running right through the earth and opening out, at the other end, in some distant part of the ocean. I mentioned this idea, as a joke – since it is foolish in the extreme – to my guide. I was surprised to hear him say that most Norwegians believed it, although he himself did not.

'You have had a good look at the whirlpool now,' he said, 'and if you come round this rock, away from the noise, I will tell you a story. It will prove to you that I ought to know something about the Moskoe-ström.'

We moved round the rock, and he continued.

'My two brothers and I once owned quite a large sailing boat, with which we were in the habit of fishing beyond Moskoe, nearly to Vurrgh. In all violent currents at sea there is good fishing, if one only has the courage to attempt it. But of all the Lofoden seamen, we three were the only ones who made a regular business of going out to the islands. The usual fishing grounds are a long way to the south. We risked going near the whirlpool because of the fine fish to be caught in large numbers around the rocks of Moskoe.

'It was our practice to sail across to the islands, far above the pool, in the fifteen minutes of calm between the tides. There we would fish until the next calm period, about six hours later, when we made our way home. We never set out without a steady wind for the journey out and our return. In six years of fishing we failed only twice to calculate the weather correctly. On both of these occasions we found safety near the islands.

'We always managed to cross the Moskoe-ström itself without accident: although at times my heart has beaten wildly when we happened to be a minute or so behind or before the calm. My oldest brother had a son of eighteen years old, and I had three strong boys of my own. These would have been a great help at such times; but, although we ran the risk ourselves, we hated the thought of taking the young ones into danger; it *was* a terrible danger, and that is the truth.

'It was almost three years ago, on 10 July 18— that we experienced along this coast the most terrible storm that ever came out of the heavens. But all morning, and even until late in the afternoon, there was a gentle and steady wind from the south-west, and not a cloud was to be seen.

'The three of us – my two brothers and myself – had crossed to the islands at about two o'clock in the afternoon. We soon loaded the boat with fine fish, which, we all agreed, were more plentiful that day than we had ever known. It was just seven, by my watch, when we started for home, so as to reach the Ström when the water was calm. We knew the calm would be at eight o'clock.

'For some time we sailed along at a great rate, never dreaming of danger, until suddenly, without any warning, the wind dropped and we could make no progress. At the same time, a

46

strange red-coloured cloud, moving at great speed, came up behind us. We had little time to wonder what to do. In less than three minutes the storm was on us, and it became so dark that we could not see each other in the boat.

'It would be foolish of me to attempt to describe that storm. The oldest seaman in Norway had never known anything like it. At its first breath, my younger brother was blown straight into the sea and lost. I would have followed him if I had not thrown myself flat, and held on to an iron ring in the middle of the boat.

'For some moments we were completely under water, and all this time I held my breath. When I could bear it no longer, I raised myself on to my knees, still holding the ring, and so got my head clear. Then our little boat gave herself a shake, just as a dog does when it comes out of the water, and got rid of some of the seawater. The next moment I felt a hand on my arm. It was my older brother, and my heart jumped for joy, since I had thought that he must have drowned. At once, though, my joy was turned into fear, as he put his mouth close to my ear and shouted out the word 'Moskoe-ström!'

'No one will ever know what my feelings were at that moment. I shook from head to foot, as if I had the most violent fever. I knew what he meant by that one word well enough – I knew what he wished to make me understand. With the wind that now drove us on, we were going straight towards the whirlpool of the Ström, and nothing could save us unless we reached it at the time of calm.

'We had lost our sails, and the boat was now out of control, racing through mountainous seas such as I had never seen in my life. A change had come over the sky, although in every direction it was still as dark as night. For a moment I was confused, but then, directly above us, a circle of clear blue sky appeared. In this circle I saw the full moon shining, lighting up everything around us – but, oh God, what a scene it was to light up!

'I now tried to speak to my brother, but he could not hear a single word; the noise had, for some reason, greatly increased. He shook his head, and held up one of his fingers, as if to say '*Listen!*' I did not quite understand what he meant.

'Suddenly a terrible thought came to me. I pulled out my watch. It was not going. I looked at its face in the moonlight, and then burst into tears as I threw it far out into the ocean. *It had stopped at seven o'clock. We had missed the period of calm, and the whirlpool of the Ström was now in full force!*

'A little later a great wave carried us with it as it rose – up – up as if into the sky; and then down we swept with a rush that made me feel sick. But while we were up, I took a quick look around – and that one look was enough. I saw our exact position immediately. The Moskoe-ström whirlpool was about a quarter of a mile in front of us. I closed my eyes with the worst feeling of fear that I have ever experienced.

'It could not have been more than two minutes afterwards when we entered the broad white belt that surrounded the centre of the whirlpool. The boat made a sharp half-turn inwards, and raced off in its new direction at great speed. The wind and the waves dropped. The thundering of the water changed to a high whistling sound – like that of a thousand steamships, all letting off their steam together. I expected, of course, that in another moment we would sink to the bottom of the whirlpool. We could not see down into the pool because of the speed with which we were carried along. The ocean that we had left now rose at our side, like an immense spinning wall between us and the horizon.

'Now that we were in the jaws of Death, I made up my mind to hope no more; and when I had reached this decision, I began to think how beautiful it was to die in such a way – surrounded, as we were, by this proof of God's power. It may seem to you that I was crazy, and perhaps I was, but I felt a wish to explore the depths of the whirlpool. My greatest sorrow was that I should never be able to tell my old companions on shore about the mysteries that I was going to see.

'How often we travelled around the edge of the pool it is impossible to say. We circled for perhaps an hour, getting gradually nearer and nearer the terrible inside edge of the white belt. Below us the water sloped away steeply. All this time I had never let go of the iron ring. My brother was now at the back of the boat, holding on to a small, empty water barrel, which was tied down tightly by a rope. This was the only thing that had not been blown away when the wind first struck us. On our last journey around the pool, before the drop into the depths, he rushed across to me. In great fear he forced my hands from the ring, and took it himself. I never felt deeper sorrow than when this happened, although I knew that it could make no difference in the end; so I let him have the ring, and went back myself to the barrel. I had hardly made myself safe in my new position, when the boat made a wild turn inwards and rushed down into the spinning depths. I said a short prayer .to God, and thought that it was all over.

'As I felt the sudden fearful drop, I tightened my hold on the barrel and closed my eyes. For some seconds I dared not open them, since I expected to be destroyed immediately. I wondered why I was not already in my death struggles with the water. About a minute passed. I was still alive. The sense of falling had gone. I took courage, and opened my eyes.

'I shall never forget the scene around me. The boat seemed to be hanging halfway down the inside surface of a circular, V-shaped hole, more than half a mile across and of immense depth. Its walls of black water, as smooth as polished wood, were spinning round with terrible speed. The light from the full moon flooded along these walls, and down to the bed of the ocean, far below.

49

'At first I was too confused to notice more than just the general view, but in a moment or two I saw that the walls of water were even steeper. The boat was resting steadily on the slope – that is to say, in her ordinary sailing position, relative to the water; and because of the great speed at which we were moving, I had no difficulty at all in holding on.

'Our first fall into the whirlpool had carried us, as I have said, about halfway down; but after that, our progress to the bottom became very much slower. Round and round we were swept, each circle taking us a yard or so lower.

'Having time to look around, I was surprised to see that our boat was not the only object that was moving. Both above and below us could be seen pieces of boats, tree trunks, and many smaller objects, such as boxes, barrels and sticks. I must have been, I think, only partly conscious at this time; for I entertained myself, while waiting for death, by trying to guess which object would be the next to fall to its destruction. "The piece of wood," I said at one time, "will certainly disappear next." And then I was disappointed to see that the wreck of a ship passed it and reached the bottom first. I had made several mistaken guesses of this kind before an idea came into my head – an idea that made me tremble again, and my heart beat heavily once more.

'It was not a new fear that I felt, but the birth of a more exciting hope. My faulty guesses had one clear meaning: a large object travelled faster down the whirlpool than a small one. It seemed possible to me, as I watched, that many of these smaller things, whose downward speed was slow, would never reach the bottom. The tide would turn, and bring the whirlpool to an end, while they were still circling its walls. They would then, I supposed, be thrown up to the surface of the ocean, and carried away by the current.

'While I considered these matters, I noticed that a short,

though very thick, tree trunk, which had been at one time on a level with us, was now high up above. Each time we passed it, the distance between us grew.

'I waited no longer. I decided to tie myself to the water barrel which I was holding, to cut it loose from the boat, and to throw myself with it into the water. As best I could, by means of signs, I explained this plan to my brother, and pointed to the floating wood that came near us. I think he understood – but, whether he did or not, he shook his head in hopelessness, and refused to move from his place by the ring. Action was now urgent; I could not afford to delay and could no longer think about him. Tying myself to the barrel by means of the rope which tied it to the boat, I rolled into the sea.

'The result was exactly what I hoped it might be. As I am now telling you this story, you see that I did escape – in the way that I have described. In the next hour our boat went down to a great distance below me. I saw it make three or four wild turns in the space of half a minute; and then, carrying my dear brother, it fell suddenly and for ever into the angry water at the bottom of the pool. The barrel to which I was tied had sunk no more than halfway to the rocks below when a great change could be seen in the sea around me. The slope of the sides of the whirlpool became, moment by moment, less and less steep. The circular movement of the water grew, gradually, less and less violent. Slowly the bottom of the well seemed to rise up towards me. The sky was clear, the wind had died down, and the full moon was setting in the west, when I floated up to the surface of the ocean. I was above the place where the whirlpool had been. It was the time of calm, but the sea was still rough from the effects of the storm. The strong current carried me away down the coast, far down to the fishing grounds. A boat picked me up; the seamen were my old companions from Lofoden, but no one recognized me. My hair, which had been black the day before, was as white as you see it now. For some time I was unable to speak (now that the danger was over) as a result of my terrible experience, but at last I told them my story. They did not believe it. I have now told it to you – and I can hardly expect *you* to believe it any more than they did.'

The Pit and the Pendulum*

After long hours of suffering, the ropes that held me were loosened, and I was allowed to sit. I felt that my senses were leaving me. I heard the judges say that I would die; these were the last sounds to reach my ears, and then the voices disappeared. I saw the black clothes of the officials, and the black curtains of the hall. The white lips of the judges moved – they were of course ordering the details of my death – and I trembled because I could hear nothing. A sudden feeling of sickness filled my body, and mist seemed to cover my eyes. Then a thought came to my mind, like a rich musical note – the thought of what sweet rest there must be in the grave. For a moment my eyes cleared, and I saw the judges stand up and leave the room; and then all was silence and stillness and night.

I had fainted; but I was not completely unconscious. In the deepest sleep, in fever, even in a dead faint, some part of consciousness remains. Long afterwards, I remembered, though not clearly, that I was lifted up from my seat in the court – that tall figures carried me in silence down – down – and still further down. At last the movement stopped, as if those who carried me could go no further. After this I remembered the cold, and my misery and great fear.

Very suddenly a sense of movement and of sound came back to me – the racing of my heart, and the sound of its beating in my ears. Then consciousness returned, and later, the power of thought. A trembling fear shook my body, and I felt a strong desire to understand my true state. I made a successful effort to

*This is a story of the Spanish Inquisition. The Inquisition was a religious court of law, which, at the time of the story, held power only in Spain. The work of the court was to find and punish people whose religious beliefs and practices did not agree with those of the Church. The punishment was often terribly severe.

move. I remembered what had happened in court – the judges, the curtains, the sentence, the sickness, my faint.

So far, I had not opened my eyes. I lay on my back, but I was not tied up. I reached out my hand, and it fell on something wet and hard. I wanted to look around, but I dared not; for I was afraid that there would be *nothing* to see. After many minutes of increasing misery, I quickly opened my eyes. The blackness of night surrounded me. I struggled for breath. The darkness seemed like a weight on me. Where and in what state was I? This was the question that troubled me. Many prisoners, I knew, were put to death in public, and such a ceremony had been held on the day that I was in court. Was I being kept until the next ceremony, which might not happen for many months?

A fearful idea now suddenly sent the blood rushing to my heart, and I trembled all over. I stood up and stretched my arms wildly above and around me in all directions. I felt nothing; but I dared not move a single step, for fear that I would be stopped by the walls of a *grave*. Taking courage at last, I moved slowly forward, with my arms in front of me. I took many steps but felt nothing. I breathed more freely; if I had been buried alive, the grave would have been smaller than this.

I went on very slowly, until my hands touched a wall; it was smooth, cold and slightly wet. I followed it, but soon realized that, without a fixed starting point, I would be unable to judge the size of the room. I now tore off a piece from the bottom of my prison clothes and placed this piece of cloth on the floor at ninety degrees to the wall. I now began to circle the room again. The ground was wet and slippery, and I had only taken a few steps when I fell forward on my face. I lay there for some minutes, and felt a great desire for sleep.

I must have slept; when I woke up, and stretched out an arm, I found beside me a loaf and a bottle of water. I ate and drank eagerly. Shortly afterwards, I continued my walk around the room, and after I had gone about fifty steps I reached the piece of cloth again. My prison, then, was about thirty yards around, if two of my steps equalled a yard.

There was little purpose – certainly no hope – in having this information; but I wanted to walk *across* the room now to get an idea of its shape. I went carefully, since the floor was very slippery. I had covered six yards, perhaps, when I fell again. Almost immediately, I noticed that although my body was resting on the floor of the prison, there seemed to be *nothing* under my head. At the same time a strange smell, like dead leaves, rose to my nose. I put out my arm, and trembled to find that I had fallen right at the edge of a circular pit. I found a small piece of loose stone, and let it fall into the hole. I listened as it struck against the sides; at last, after many seconds, it hit water. A faint beam of light flashed suddenly in the roof above me, and there was a sound like the quick opening and closing of a door. And then all was darkness again.

I now knew what had been prepared for me. If I had taken one more step before my fall, the world would never have seen me again. The death that I had avoided was just the kind of death which I had heard of in stories about the Inquisition. I had laughed at those stories; I had thought of them as wild and imaginary. But I now knew that they were true. The Inquisition offered a choice of death: one could die in great physical pain or by the most terrible mental suffering. And death in the pit would come to me slowly, through the destruction of my mind.

I struggled back to the wall. Shaking violently, I imagined other holes in the ground in various positions in the room, and other hidden forms of punishment. Thoughts such as these kept me awake for many hours, but at last I slept again. When I awoke, I found another bottle of water and some bread beside me. I drank the water immediately, as I was very thirsty. It must have contained something to make me sleep, and I could not keep my eyes open. My state of unconsciousness must have lasted a long time; but when, once again, I awoke, I could see the objects around me. A bright yellow light shone into my prison, though I could not see where it came from.

The room was roughly square, and of about the size that I had calculated. But the walls, which I had thought were made of stone, seemed now to be iron or some other kind of metal, in very large plates. The whole surface of this metal room was painted with the figures of devils in the most terrible shapes. Although their forms were clear enough, the colours seemed to have become paler, as if from the effects of the wet air. The floor was of stone, and in its centre was the circular pit into which I had so nearly fallen. It was the only pit.

I saw all this only by much effort – for my situation had changed greatly during my sleep. I now lay on my back, at full length, on a kind of low bed. I was tied to this tightly and was free to move only my head and the lower part of my left arm. I could just manage to reach the food which lay beside me on the floor. The water had gone – and I was more thirsty than ever.

Looking upwards, I examined the roof of my prison. It was thirty or forty feet above, and was also made of metal. Directly over my bed the figure of Father Time was painted on one of the plates. When I first looked at this picture, I thought that the figure held in his hand a large pendulum, such as we see on old clocks. But a moment later the pendulum moved, and I realized that it was not a part of the picture. The movement was short and slow – a slight swing from side to side. I watched it with interest for a few minutes, and then turned my attention to other parts of the room.

I heard noises, and saw several large rats crossing the floor towards me. They had come out of the pit which lay on my right side. As I watched, they came up in large numbers, hurrying, with hungry-looking eyes, towards my plate of food.

It required a great deal of effort and attention to frighten them away.

It might have been half an hour, perhaps even an hour, before I looked up to the roof again. What I saw there confused me. The swing of the pendulum had increased to almost a yard. As a natural result of this, its speed was now much greater. But what mainly disturbed me was the fact that it had come nearer. In great fear, I saw that the lower end of the pendulum was formed of a blade of shining steel, shaped like the new moon, and about a foot in length from point to point. The ends of the blade turned upwards; and the lower edge looked as sharp as a sword. It was fixed to a thick bar of iron, and the whole blade whistled as it swung through the air.

I could no longer doubt the death that had been prepared for me by the human devils of the Inquisition. I had avoided the pit by chance, and I knew that surprise was an important part of the cruelty of these prison deaths. As I had failed to fall, I was not simply to be thrown into the well. A different and a gentler destruction was made ready for me. Gentler! I trembled as I thought about the word.

What use is it to tell of the long, long hours of suffering that followed, during which I counted the swings of the steel? Slowly it fell – down and still down it came! The downward movement was extremely slow, and it was only after several hours that I noticed any increase in the length of the iron bar. Days passed – it might have been many days – before the blade swept so close that it seemed to blow me with its bitter breath. The smell of the sharp steel came to me in waves. I prayed for it to reach me quickly. I struggled to force myself upwards against the sharp edge, as it swung across my body. And then I grew suddenly calm, and lay smiling at the shining death, as a child smiles at a bright jewel.

For a short time I lost consciousness. When my senses returned, I felt sick and weak; but in spite of my suffering, I wanted food. With painful effort I reached for the few pieces of meat beside me. As I put some of it to my lips, a half-formed thought of joy – of hope – rushed into my mind. I struggled to make it complete, but it escaped me. Long suffering had nearly killed all my ordinary powers of mind.

The swing of the pendulum was across my body – directly across my heart. It would first touch the cloth of my prison clothes; it would return and cut deeper – again – and again. In spite of its wide swing (which was now thirty feet or more), and its great force, it would not, for several minutes, cut into my flesh. At this thought, I paused. I dared not think further. I watched the blade as it flew above me.

Down – steadily down it came. To the right – to the left – far and wide – with the terrible *whistle* of death! Down – certainly down just above my chest! I struggled violently to free my left arm. I shook and turned my head at every swing. I opened and closed my eyes as the bright blade flashed above me. Oh, if I could die!

Suddenly I felt the calmness of hopelessness flood through me. For the first time in many hours – or perhaps days – I began to think. The band which tied me was in one piece; but I saw immediately that no part of this lay across my chest. There was no hope, then, that the steel would cut the band, and set me free. If, though, the band were broken at one point, I could quickly unwind it from the rest of my body, and slide off the bed. But how terribly close the blade would be! And how difficult the slightest movement would be, beneath that knife of destruction!

Suddenly the unformed half of that thought of hope (that I have already mentioned) came into my mind. The whole idea was now present – weak, unreasonable perhaps – but complete. I immediately began my attempt to escape death.

The rats, I hoped, would save me. For many hours they had surrounded my bed. They were wild and hungry, and they had, in the short time that I lay unconscious, eaten nearly all the meat on the plate. 'Where do they usually get their food from,' I wondered, 'in this place?'

For a long time I had kept my left arm moving, to frighten them away, and many had bitten my fingers in their efforts to reach the plate. I knew that if I lay still they would rush on me. I now took the last pieces of the rich oily meat from the plate, and rubbed them thoroughly into the band wherever I could reach it. Then, resting my hand on the bed, I lay perfectly still.

In a moment one or two of the biggest jumped on to the bed, and smelt at the band. This seemed the signal for a general rush. Out of the pit they came in fresh numbers; they climbed on the bed, and I was soon covered by hundreds of rats. The movement of the pendulum did not disturb them at all. Avoiding its strokes, they tore the band into which I had rubbed the meat. They pressed over me. I felt their cold lips against mine; I could hardly breathe for their weight. A terrible sick feeling, for which there is no name, swelled my body, and brought a coldness to my heart. One minute more, and I felt the struggle would be over. I noticed the loosening of the band. I knew that in more than one place it must already be broken. I lay still.

I had made no mistake – and I had not suffered for nothing. At last I felt that I was free. The band hung in pieces from my body. But the pendulum had already cut through my clothes. Twice more it swung, and a sharp pain ran through my body. But now the moment of escape had arrived. At a wave of my hand, the rats hurried away. With a steady movement – careful, sideways, slow – I rolled from the bed and beyond the reach of the blade. For the moment, at least, I was free.

Free – but in the hands of the Inquisition! I had hardly moved from my bed of suffering on to the stone floor, when the movement of the terrible machine stopped, and it was pulled up, by some unseen force, through the roof. I now realized that every action of mine was being watched. I had only escaped death in one form to suffer it in another! I looked anxiously around the walls of my iron prison. Something unusual – a change, which, at first, I could not understand, had taken place. While I wondered about this, I saw the origin of the yellow light which filled the room. It came from a narrow space which ran around the whole room at the base of the walls. The walls were completely separated from the floor. I tried, but of course I failed, to look through this crack.

As I got up from the floor, the mystery of the change in the room suddenly became clear. The terrible figures on the walls – the paintings whose colours, as I have said, seemed to have become less definite – now stood out as brightly as living creatures! Their wild eyes shone with fire – real fire; as I breathed, the smell of heated iron reached my senses. The walls grew hot and began to burn. I struggled for breath, and rushed to the centre of the room. I thought of the coldness of the pit, and I looked down into its depth. It was lit up by the fire of the burning roof. For a moment, though, I refused to believe what I saw in that well of death. Oh! for a voice to speak! – oh! the cruelty of it! Any death – but not the pit! With a cry, I turned from its edge and buried my face in my hands.

The heat rapidly increased. I was soon forced to look up again; and when I did so, it was to see that the iron walls were moving. Two opposite corners of the room were growing slowly further apart – while the distance between the other pair got smaller. The prison was now diamond-shaped and quickly becoming flatter and flatter. 'Death,' I said, 'any death, but not the pit!' Fool! I should have guessed that it was the whole object of those moving walls of fire to force me into the pit. Could I bear their heat? Could I bear their pressure?

At last I knew that I could not. The closing walls pressed me to the side of the well. There was no longer any foothold for my burnt and twisting body on the firm floor of the prison. I struggled no more, but gave one long, loud and terrible shout of hopelessness. I felt that I trembled on the edge – I closed my eyes – there was a sound of human voices! There was the music of victory! The fiery walls rushed back! A strong arm caught my own as I fell, fainting, into the pit. It was that of General Lasalle. The French army had entered the city of Toledo. The Inquisition was in the hands of its enemies.

The Stolen Letter

In Paris, just after dark, one windy evening in the autumn of 18—, I was enjoying a quiet smoke with my friend C. Auguste Dupin, at his home in Faubourg St-Germain. We had been together for at least an hour, when our old friend, Monsieur* G—, the head of the Paris police, called to see Dupin.

We welcomed him warmly, since we found his presence highly entertaining, and we had not seen him for some time. We had been sitting in the dark, and Dupin now got up to light a lamp. He sat down again immediately, though, when G— said that he had called to ask for advice about some official business which had caused him a great deal of trouble.

'If it is something which requires thought,' said Dupin, 'we shall consider it with more success in the dark.'

'That is another of your strange ideas,' said the officer, who had a habit of calling everything 'strange' that was beyond his power of understanding. He lived in a world of 'strange' events.

'Very true,' said Dupin, as he gave his visitor a pipe, and pushed a comfortable chair towards him.

'And what is the difficulty now?' I asked. 'No one has been murdered, I hope?'

'Oh no; nothing of that kind. The business is very simple, and I have no doubt that we can manage it quite well ourselves; but I thought that Dupin would like to hear the details of it, because it is so very strange.'

'Simple and strange,' said Dupin.

'Well, yes; but not exactly that, either. The fact is we have all been extremely confused because the affair is so simple, but it has completely defeated us.'

*Monsieur: the French word for *Mr*.

62

'Perhaps it is the simplicity of the problem that makes it so difficult for the police,' said my friend.

'What nonsense you do talk!' replied G—, laughing loudly.

'Perhaps the mystery is a little *too* plain,' said Dupin.

'Well, well! Who ever heard of such an idea?'

'And what, after all, *is* the trouble?' I asked.

'I will tell you,' replied the officer, as he filled his pipe, and settled himself into his chair. 'I will tell you in a few words. But before I begin, let me warn you that this is an affair of the greatest secrecy. I would almost certainly lose my position, if it became known that I had told it to anyone.'

'Go on,' I said.

'Or not,' said Dupin.

'Well, then; I have received personal information, from a very high place, that a certain letter of great importance has been taken from the royal rooms. The person who took it is known; this is beyond doubt, since he was seen taking it. It is known, too, that it still remains in his possession.'

'How is this known?' asked Dupin.

'It is known because certain things would immediately happen if the letter passed out of the robber's possession; that is to say, if he employed it in the way that he must be planning, in the end, to employ it. These things have not yet happened.'

'Give us more details,' I said.

'Well, I may say that the paper gives its holder a certain power in certain circles where such power is of immense value.' G— was very fond of this official way of speaking.

'I still do not quite understand,' said Dupin.

'No? Well, if a third person, who shall be nameless, should learn what is in the letter, then the honour of another person of the very highest rank would be in doubt. So the holder of the letter has power over the respected person whose honour and peace of mind are in danger.'

'But this power,' I said, 'would be useless without full knowledge on both sides. I mean that the loser of the letter would have to know who had stolen it, and the thief would have to know that he was known. Who would dare—'

'The thief,' said G—, 'is the Minister D—, who dares do anything. The letter had been received by the person to whom it was addressed, while she was alone in her sitting room. While she was reading it, the other person – the one who, as I have said, shall be nameless – entered the room. The lady wished especially to hide the letter from him, but she had no time to do so. She was forced to place it, open as it was, on a table; but the address was face up, and the letter itself escaped notice. At this moment the Minister D— entered. His sharp eye immediately saw the paper, recognized the handwriting of the address, and noticed the lady's confusion. He guessed her secret. After some business matters had been completed, D— took out a letter from his pocket, opened it, pretended to read it, and then placed it close to the other on the table. He then continued, for another quarter of an hour, to discuss public affairs. Finally, as he was leaving, he took the lady's letter, and left his own – one of no importance – on the table. The lady saw all this, but, of course, dared not say anything in the presence of the third person who stood beside her.'

'Here, then,' said Dupin to me, 'you have full knowledge on both sides, and D— has the lady in his power. She saw him take the letter, and he knows that she saw him.'

'Yes,' said the officer; 'and the power gained in this way has been used, for some months past, for political purposes, to a very dangerous degree. It becomes clearer to the lady every day that she must get her letter back. But this cannot be done openly, of course. She has come to me to ask for my help.'

'As you are the wisest adviser, I suppose,' said Dupin, 'whom she could desire or even imagine.'

'It is possible that she has that opinion,' replied G—.

'It is clear,' I said, 'that the minister will try to keep the letter. If he destroyed it, he would lose his power over the lady. We must believe that he still has it.'

'Exactly,' said the officer. I feel so sure that he still has it that I have made a thorough search of his home. It was not easy, because I had to search in secret. I have been warned that it would be very dangerous for me if the minister suspected our plans.'

'But the Paris police know very well how to search a house in secret,' I said. 'They have done this thing often before.'

'Oh yes; and for this reason I did not give up hope. The habits of the minister, too, gave me a great advantage. He is frequently absent from home all night. He has few servants, and they sleep at a distance from their master's rooms. I have keys, as you know, with which I can open any door in Paris. Every night for three months I have personally directed the search. I have promised on my honour to get this letter back; and, although it is a secret, I can tell you that the reward is immense. So I did not give up the search until I was sure that I had examined every hiding place in the house.'

'Well, then,' I suggested, 'the letter may not be hidden in the house at all.'

'It probably *is* in the house,' said Dupin. 'D— might have to produce it at a moment's notice.'

'Have you searched the minister himself?' I asked.

'Yes; my men, pretending to be robbers, have twice searched him thoroughly.'

'That was hardly necessary,' said Dupin. 'D— is not a complete fool. He would have expected something like that to happen.'

'Not a complete fool,' said the officer, 'but he's a poet, and so little better than a fool.'

'True,' said Dupin, sucking thoughtfully on his pipe.

'Tell us,' I said, 'the details of your search.'

'Well, the fact is that we searched thoroughly. We took the whole building, room by room, and spent the nights of a whole week in each. We examined the furniture first. We opened every possible drawer; and I suppose you know that, to a properly trained police officer, such a thing as a secret drawer is impossible. There is a certain amount of space to be accounted for in every desk or cupboard. Next we took the chairs, and we examined the seats with the fine long needles which you have seen me use. Then we took the tops of the tables off.'

'Why?' said Dupin.

'To see if there was anything hidden in the legs. The bottoms and tops of bedposts are often used as hiding places in the same way.'

'But surely you did not take the furniture to pieces completely? A letter may be rolled up tightly, and pressed into a small hole, for example, in the back of a chair.'

'We examined every part of every piece of furniture. If there had been any small holes or changes to the design, we would not have failed to see them immediately. The smallest grain of wood dust would have been as clear to us as an apple.'

I suppose you looked at the beds and bedclothes, the curtains and the floor coverings.'

'Of course; and when we had finished these things, we examined the house itself – every piece of every floor and wall, both inside and outside.'

'You must have had a great deal of trouble,' I said.

'We did; but the reward offered is great.'

'Did you include the grounds of the house?'

'All the grounds are covered in brick. They gave us little trouble. We examined the soil between the bricks, and found no sign that they had been moved.'

'You looked among D——'s papers, of course, and among the books in his library?'

'Certainly; we not only opened every book, but we turned over every page. We also measured the thickness of every book cover, and examined each very carefully.'

'You checked the paper on the walls?'

'We did.'

'Then,' I said, 'you have made a mistake, and the letter is not in the house, as you believed.'

'I do not know what to think,' said G——. 'Now, Dupin, what do you advise me to do?'

'To search the house thoroughly again.'

'But that is clearly unnecessary,' replied G——. 'As sure as I breathe, the letter is not there.'

'I have no better advice to give you,' said Dupin. 'You have, of course, a full description of the letter?'

'Oh yes!' – And here the officer, taking a notebook from his pocket, read aloud a detailed account of the appearance of the letter. When he had finished this, he left us, lower in spirits than I had ever known him before.

About a month afterwards he called on Dupin again, and found us sitting in the darkness, smoking, as before. He took a pipe and a chair, and began some ordinary conversation. After a little time, I said: 'Well, G——, what about the stolen letter? Has the minister defeated you?'

'I am afraid that he has. I searched again, as Dupin suggested; it was wasted work, as I knew it would be.'

'How much was the reward, did you say?' asked Dupin.

'A very great deal – a very generous reward – I don't like to say how much, exactly. The matter is becoming more and more urgent every day; and the reward has recently been doubled. If it were doubled again, though, I could do no more than I have done.'

'Oh, you might, I think, do a little more.'

'How? – in what way?'

'Well, you might employ a good lawyer, for example. Do you remember the story of Abernethy, the doctor?'

'No; what is it?'

'Well, once there was a certain rich old man who tried to get a free medical opinion from Abernethy. He began an ordinary conversation with the doctor, and pretended that the case was an imaginary one. 'We will suppose,' said the rich old man, 'that the man is suffering from …' (and here the old man mentioned the name of his disease); 'now, doctor, what would you have ordered him to take?'

'Take!' said Abernethy. 'Why, take advice, of course.'

'But,' said the officer, a little uncomfortable, 'I do want to take advice, and to pay for it. I would give half the reward to anyone who would help me in the matter.'

'In that case,' replied Dupin, opening a drawer, and taking out a chequebook, 'you may as well write a cheque for me for that amount. When you have signed it, I will give you the letter.'

I could not hide my surprise. But G— plainly did not believe what he had heard. For some minutes he could not speak; he looked at Dupin with open mouth and wide eyes. At last he seized a pen, and, after several pauses, wrote out and signed a cheque, which he handed across the table to Dupin. My friend examined it carefully, and put it in his pocket. Then, unlocking the drawer of a desk, Dupin took out a letter and gave it to the officer. G— took it quickly, opened it with a trembling hand, and read the message. Then he rushed to the door, and out of the room, without saying a single word.

When he had gone, my friend gave me an explanation.

'The Paris police,' he said, 'are very clever in the ordinary way. They are patient and careful, and these qualities usually bring results. They have one weakness, though, and G— is, himself, an excellent example of this: they have no imagination. They never try to imagine what is in the mind of their enemy. Whatever the case, and whoever the enemy, the actions of the police are always the same. G— and his people frequently fall, first, because they do not try to get inside the mind of the wrongdoer; and second, because they do not measure properly the skill of the enemy. So when they are searching for anything hidden, they think only of the ways in which *they* would have hidden it. G— believes that anyone who wanted to hide a letter would hide it in one or other of the places where he searched: if not in a table leg, then in the back of a chair, or under the floorboards, or perhaps inside the cover of a book. Now in this case, the police failed really because G— considered that the minister was a fool; and he considered him a fool because he is a poet.'

'But is D— really a poet?' I asked. 'There are two brothers, I know; and both are well educated. The minister, I believe, has written a good deal on scientific subjects. He is a scientist, and not a poet.'

'You are wrong; I know him well, and he is both. As a poet and a scientist, he would be able to reason well. If he had simply been a scientist, he could not have reasoned at all, and would have been at the mercy of the police.'

'You surprise me,' I said, 'with these opinions; but we had better discuss them at some other time. I am very interested now in how you found the letter. Go on.'

'Well, I know D—, both as scientist and as a poet, and I considered him also to be a good politician and a gentleman of the Court. Such a man would expect the police to search his house. I believe that he stayed away from his home at night on purpose – to give the police the opportunity for a thorough search, so that they would decide at last that the letter was not in the building. D—, you see, knew where they would search. He knew that his furniture would be taken to pieces, and that they would look into the smallest and darkest corner of his home. It seemed to me that the minister would be forced to find a simple hiding place for the letter. You will remember, perhaps, how loudly G— laughed when I suggested at the beginning that it was possibly the simplicity of the problem that made it so difficult for him.'

'Yes,' I said, 'I remember very well. He seemed to think that you were joking.'

'I was not joking,' said Dupin. 'Some things are too plain for us to see. There is a game that children are fond of, which is played on a map. One player asks the others to find a certain word – the name of a town, river or state – that is shown somewhere on the map. Now most children choose a name that is written in very small letters, since they think that such a word is harder to find. But a good player chooses a word that stretches, in large letters, right across the map – a word that is so plain, in fact, that it escapes notice. It is the same with shop signs in the street. We stop and struggle to read every letter of the small ones, but hardly look at the big ones. Our friend G— never thought that the letter would be right under his nose; he never thought that the minister could hide the letter in the best way by not hiding it at all.

'Such a trick, it seemed to me, completely suited the daring character of the minister; and I decided to prove that my idea was right. Wearing a pair of dark glasses, I called one morning at D—'s house. He was at home, pretending to be tired and too lazy to work, although he is really one of the busiest men in Paris.

'Choosing a similar pretence, I complained of my weak eyes, and that I had to wear glasses. While we talked, I looked carefully around the room, but at the same time paid proper attention to the conversation.

'I was very interested in a large writing table, near which the minister sat. A number of papers and letters, several books and a musical instrument lay on it; but after a long and detailed

70

examination of this, from where I sat, I could see nothing to cause suspicion.

'At last my eyes, travelling around the room, fell on an ordinary letter holder, made of wire. This hung by a dirty blue string from a small metal hook just above the fireplace. In this holder were five or six visiting cards and one letter. The letter was dirty, and torn across the middle – as if someone had started to tear it up, but had then decided to keep it. A large stamp showed the arms of the D— family very clearly. The letter was addressed, in small female handwriting, to the minister himself. It had been pushed carelessly into the top of the holder.

'This,' I said to myself immediately, 'is what I have come for.' The appearance of the letter was quite different from that of the missing one. But these details – the stamp, the address and the handwriting – could easily result from a simple change of envelope. The dirty and torn condition of the letter, and the careless way in which it lay in the holder, were quite unlike the ordinary tidy habits of D—. I believed that these things might be a part of his plan to deceive the police. When I thought of all this, and saw the letter in full view of every visitor, I had no serious doubts. As soon as I could politely end our conversation, I said goodbye to the minister and went home. I left my gold cigarette box on the table.

'The next morning I called for the cigarette box, and talked to D for several minutes. Suddenly a gunshot was heard outside the house, followed by a loud cry and the shouts of a crowd. D— rushed to the window, threw it open and looked out. I stepped to the letter holder, took out the letter, and put it in my pocket. I put another in its place, exactly like it in appearance, which I had carefully prepared at home. Then I followed D— to the window.

'The trouble in the street had been caused by the behaviour of a man who had fired an old gun among a crowd of women and children. When the gun was examined, it was found to have powder in it but no shot, and the man was allowed to go free. Soon afterwards I left D—'s house. A little later I met the man with the gun, and paid him what I had promised him.'

'But why,' I asked, 'did you put another letter into the holder?'

'You know my political views,' replied Dupin. In this matter. I am on the lady's side. For eighteen months the minister has had her in his power. She now has him in hers, since it may be several weeks, or even months, before D— discovers that he no longer possesses the letter. During this time he will continue to act towards the lady as if the letter were still in his letter holder. Sooner or later she will be able to trap him and cause his political destruction. I have no sympathy for the minister – nor for any clever man who is without honour. I must say, though, that I would like to know D—'s thoughts when at last he is forced to open the letter which I placed in his letter holder.'

'Why? Did you write any particular message?'

'Well, it did not seem proper to leave no message at all – that would have been insulting. In Vienna, many years ago, D— acted rather badly towards me, and I told him, quite pleasantly, that I would remember it. He will wonder who it is who has defeated him; so I decided to help him a little. He knows my handwriting well, and I just wrote in the middle of an empty page the words:

'A trick so daring
Requires one more daring to better it.'

Metzengerstein

Strange and terrible events can happen at any time. Why, then, should I give a date to this story? It is enough to say that, at that time, the country people of Hungary held strong beliefs about the human soul. They believed that a soul lived once only in a human body; and that, after death, it passed into the living body of an animal.

The old families of Berlifitzing and Metzengerstein had been enemies for centuries. The origin of the quarrel seems to be found in the words of an old saying: 'A great name shall have a fearful fall when Metzengerstein shall defeat and be defeated by Berlifitzing.' The words themselves had little or no meaning – but equally eventful results have come from more foolish origins than this.

The two families were close neighbours, and they had, for a long time, taken opposite sides in the affairs of a busy government. The high towers of the Castle Berlifitzing, home of the younger and less wealthy family, looked directly into the windows of the Palace of Metzengerstein. One might say that the quarrel was kept alive, and the two houses kept apart, mainly by their nearness to each other.

William von Berlifitzing was, at the time of this story, a sick and stupid old man. Two feelings kept him alive: a deep hatred for the Metzengerstein name, and a great love of horses and of hunting. Neither sickness, great age, nor weakness of mind prevented him from taking part, every day, in the dangers of the hunt.

Frederick von Metzengerstein was, on the other hand, not yet twenty-one years of age. His father, the Minister G—, died young. His mother, Lady Mary, followed him quickly. Frederick was at that time eighteen years old. In a city, eighteen years are nothing; but in the wild countryside – in so grand a country as this one – time has a deeper meaning.

The Metzengerstein possessions were the richest in Hungary.

The borders of the largest park stretched more than fifty miles, and there were many castles, of which the Palace of Metzengerstein was the grandest. When his father died and Frederick arrived at the Palace to take control of his property, he soon showed his trembling servants, and the quiet country people of the area, that he was as bad as he was wild. For three days and nights the wine flowed freely. The shameful behaviour and terrible cruelty of the new master reached its lowest point in the evening of the fourth day, when the stables of the Castle Berlifitzing were found to be on fire.

While they burned, Frederick sat alone deep in thought in one of the upper rooms of the Palace. Great pictures of his ancient family looked down on him. Here, a group of richly dressed priests, sitting with one of the Metzengersteins, shook a warning finger at a king, or laughed in the face of a threatening Berlifitzing. There, the tall, dark figures of the Metzengerstein princes, on their warhorses, stood in victory over the bodies of their enemies.

As Frederick listened to the noises of the fire, his eyes turned by chance to the picture of a great red horse. The animal seemed to fill the picture; its rider, who appeared only in the background, had fallen by the sword of a Metzengerstein. The dying horseman, whose killer stood over him was, Frederick knew, a member of the other family.

An evil expression came to the young man's face, as he looked at the scene. After a while he tried to look away, but for some reason his eyes refused to obey him. A feeling of great anxiety came over him, and the longer he looked, the more anxious he became. The noise outside grew suddenly more violent. Frederick forced himself to look at the bright light of the fire which was shining through the windows.

But only for a moment; his eyes then returned immediately to the picture on the wall. To his surprise and fear, he noticed that the head of the great horse had changed its position. Before, it had been lowered, as if in pity, over the body of its rider; now it was stretched at full length towards Frederick himself. The large red eyes wore an almost human expression, and the whole appearance of the animal suggested strong anger.

Shaking with fear, the young man ran to the door. As he threw it open, a flash of red light from the window threw his own shadow onto the picture – and it exactly covered the figure of that ancient Metzengerstein prince, the victorious killer of the Berlifitzing horseman.

Frederick rushed into the open air. At the palace gates he met three servants who, with much difficulty and at great risk, were struggling to control the wild movements of a great red horse.

'Whose horse? Where did you get him?' cried the young man, as he saw immediately that it was exactly like the horse in the picture.

'He is your own property, sir,' replied one of the men; 'at least, no one else claims him. We caught him flying, blowing and smoking with anger, from the burning stables of the Castle Berlifitzing. Thinking that he belonged to the old man, we led him back there. But they say that he is not one of theirs; which is strange, for he bears clear marks of a narrow escape from the flames. The letters W V B are burnt on to his head, and of course I thought that they meant William von Berlifitzing – but no one at the castle has any knowledge of the horse.'

'Very strange,' said the young man. 'He is, though, a fine horse and an unusual one. Let him be mine, then. Perhaps a rider like Frederick von Metzengerstein can drive out even the devil from the stables of Berlifitzing.'

At that moment another servant stepped quickly out of the doorway of the Palace. He whispered in his master's ear an account of the sudden disappearance of a large part of one of the pictures in an upper room. Frederick felt the return of all the strange anxieties that had troubled him earlier, and once again a look of the deepest evil came over his face. He gave orders that the room should be locked up immediately, and the key handed to him.

'Have you heard of the unhappy death of the old hunter Berlifitzing?' said one of the men, as the servant went back into the Palace, and the great horse was led away to Frederick's stable.

'No!' said the young lord, turning quickly towards the speaker. 'Dead, you say?'

'It is true, sir; and, to someone with your name, the news will not be unwelcome, I think.'

A quick smile appeared on Frederick's face. 'How did he die?'

'In a foolish attempt to save one of his favourite horses. He died in the flames.'

'Well, well!' said the young man, as if the truth of an exciting idea was slowly entering his mind. 'Terrible!' said the youth calmly, and turned quietly into the Palace.

From that time a noticeable change was seen in the behaviour of the young Frederick von Metzengerstein. He never went beyond the borders of his own land. He kept none of his old friends, and made no new ones – unless that wild, unnatural red horse, which he was always riding, could be called a friend. He refused to attend social events in the neighbourhood, and took no interest in local affairs. After a time, the invitations that were sent to him became less friendly and less frequent. In the end they stopped altogether.

The more generous people thought that young Frederick was unhappy because of the early death of his parents; they forgot his terrible behaviour of the first few days. Others believed that he was too proud to mix with his less wealthy neighbours. The family doctor spoke of an unhealthy sadness, from which other members of the family had suffered. There were a few who thought the young man was crazy, and certainly Frederick's strange love for the great red horse showed a very unhealthy state of mind. This love seemed to grow stronger as the animal gave fresh proof of its wild nature. In the heat of midday – at the darkest hour of night – in sickness or in health – in calm or in storm – the young Metzengerstein was for ever on the back of that immense creature.

The speed of the animal, said the villagers, was twice that of any other horse. It was a strange thing that no one – except the young lord – had ever touched the body of the animal. Even the three men who had caught him, as he ran from the burning stables, had done so by means of a long chain around his neck. No one, except the master, was allowed to look after the horse, whose stable was some distance from the rest. And no one minded this, because people said that Metzengerstein himself turned pale, and stepped back, when the eyes of the horse shone with a bright and terrible light – a human light, deep and searching.

Among all the servants at the Palace, none doubted the great love which existed between their master and this nameless animal; none, that is, except a young boy, whose opinions were not at all important. This boy was foolish enough to say that Metzengerstein never climbed onto the horse without a slight trembling of the body. The boy also said that when his master returned from every long ride, a look of victorious evil twisted every feature of his face.

One stormy night Metzengerstein woke from a heavy sleep and rushed from his room to the stables. He lumped onto the horse and raced away into the depths of the forest. This sort of behaviour was quite common and attracted no particular attention, but when he had been absent for several hours, the servants discovered that the Palace of Metzengerstein was on fire. Soon the great walls were cracking and falling in a heat which was impossible to control. A large part of the building had already been destroyed by the time the flames were first seen. And now the local people could do nothing but stand and watch in silence.

Suddenly, up the long drive which led from the forest to the main entrance of the Palace, a horse and rider flew at a speed never before seen on earth. The horseman struggled with all his strength to control the animal. His face was a picture of pain; but no sound came from his lips, which were bitten through in his terrible fear. One moment the sound of the horse's feet rang out above the noise of the flames and the crashing of the storm; the next, both horse and rider rushed into the flaming building, and far up the staircase into the white heat of the fire.

The wind immediately grew calm. The building still burned, and suddenly a stream of light shot up into the quiet air. A cloud of smoke settled over the Palace in the clear, immense figure of – a *horse*.

The Murders in the Rue Morgue

During the spring and part of the summer of 18—, my friend C. Auguste Dupin and I shared a house in Paris, in a quiet part of the Faubourg St-Germain. It was our habit, at this time, to stay indoors for most of the day, and to take long walks after dark through the wild lights and shadows of the busy city. We gained a good deal of quiet enjoyment from this simple pleasure. It was in darkness (as I have noted in a previous story) that Dupin found his mind most active, his power of reasoning at its best, and his ability to notice things around him extremely sharp.

We were walking one night down a long dirty street on the east side of the city. We were both, it seemed, deep in thought; neither of us had spoken a word for at least fifteen minutes. Then suddenly Dupin broke the silence with these words: 'He is a very little man, that's true, and would be more suited to a lighter or more humorous play.'

'There is no doubt about that,' I replied, not at first noticing the strange way in which Dupin had followed my thoughts. But a moment later I realized and felt most surprised.

'Dupin,' I said, seriously, 'I do not understand this at all. I can hardly believe my ears. How did you know that I was thinking about...?' Here I paused, to see if he could complete my question.

'...about the actor, Chantilly,' he said. 'You were thinking that he is too physically small for a serious play.'

I must admit that that was exactly the subject of my thoughts. Chantilly was a shoemaker, who had suddenly become interested in acting. He had attempted the part of King Xerxes in the play of that name and the papers had criticized him severely.

'Tell me,' I cried, 'how you have been able to reach into my mind like this.'

'It was the fruit seller,' replied my friend, 'who made you feel sure that Chantilly was not tall enough for Xerxes.'

'The fruit seller! – you surprise me – I know of no fruit seller.'

'The man who nearly pushed you over as we entered the street – it may have been fifteen minutes ago.'

I now remembered that, in fact, a tradesman who was carrying a large basket of apples on his head had struck against me by accident, as we passed into the street where we now were. But I could not possibly understand how this was connected with Chantilly.

'I will explain,' said Dupin, 'so that you will understand it all clearly. We had been talking of horses, I believe, just before turning the corner. This was our last subject of discussion. As we turned into this street, the fruit seller pushed you onto a pile of stones, which stood at a place where the road is being repaired. You stepped on a broken piece, slipped, and twisted your foot slightly. You turned to look at the pile, appeared to be a little annoyed, and then continued in silence. I was not paying particular attention to what you did, but I happened to notice some of your actions.

'You kept your eyes on the ground, and soon we came to a part of the road where the new stones had already been laid in a rather strange pattern. This pattern reminded me of an old Greek idea of the positions of certain stars in the heavens. And, as we discussed this subject not very long ago, I thought that you would be reminded of it too. I felt that you could not avoid looking up at the stars. You did look up; and I was now quite sure that I had followed your thoughts. But in that bitter attack on Chantilly, which appeared in yesterday's newspaper, the writer said that he was "a falling star which shines for a moment, and is then gone for ever". Just then, as you were looking up, a star moved quickly across the sky. It was clear, therefore, that you would connect the star with Chantilly. I saw a little smile pass over your lips, as you thought of the poor shoemaker's failure. Until then you had bent forward as you walked; but now I saw you straighten yourself to your full height. And I was certain that you were thinking of the shortness of Chantilly. At that moment I said that, as he was a very little man, he would do better in a lighter play.'

Not long after this conversation, we were reading an evening newspaper, when the following paragraph caught our attention:

MYSTERIOUS MURDERS

At about three o'clock this morning, people living in the rue★ Morgue were woken by terrible cries which came from the fourth-floor flat of Madame★ L'Espanaye and her daughter, Mademoiselle★ Camille L'Espanaye. After breaking open the street door, which was locked, eight or ten of the neighbours entered, with two policemen. By this time the cries had stopped. As the party rushed up the stairs, two or more rough voices were heard, arguing angrily. The sounds seemed to come from the upper part of the house. As the second floor was reached, these sounds also stopped, and everything remained quiet. The party hurried from room to room. They had to force the door of a large back room on the third floor, which was found locked with the key on the inside. A terrible sight then met their eyes.

The room was in great disorder; the furniture broken and thrown about in all directions. On one of the chairs lay an open razor, covered with blood. Two or three handfuls of thick grey human hair lay near the fireplace. This hair seemed to have been pulled out by the roots, since small pieces of flesh were sticking to it. On the floor the party found four gold coins, an earring, three large silver spoons, and two bags, containing nearly 4,000 gold coins. The drawers of a desk were open and seemed to have been searched, although many things still remained in them.

★*rue; Madame; Mademoiselle*: the French words for *street; Mrs; Miss*.

There was no sign of Madame L'Espanaye. But, as the fireplace was unusually dirty and much disturbed, the chimney was examined. The body of the daughter, head downwards, was dragged from it. It had been forced up the narrow opening for several feet. The body was quite warm. The skin had broken, probably by the violence with which it had been pushed up and pulled down. There were deep cuts on the face, and clear marks of fingernails around the neck. It looked as if the girl had been killed by the pressure of human hands around her throat.

After a thorough search of every part of the flat, the party went downstairs and into a small yard at the back of the building. There they found the body of the old lady, with her throat cut. In fact, it was so completely cut that the head fell off as soon as they tried to lift her.

So far nothing has been found which might help to solve this terrible mystery.

The next day's papers gave this further information.

THE MURDERS IN THE RUE MORGUE

Many people have now been questioned about this crime, but the police have discovered nothing which might help them to solve it. We give below information from statements that have been made by witnesses.

Pauline Dubourg said that she had known Madame L'Espanaye and her daughter for three years, during which time she had done their washing. The two ladies seemed to be very close and loving companions. Paid well. Seemed to have money in the bank. Never met anyone in the house when she called for the clothes or took them back. Was sure that they had no servant. The lower floors of the building appeared not to be used.

Pierre Moreau, tobacconist, said that he had sold small quantities of tobacco to Madame L'Espanaye for nearly four years. The two ladies had lived in the house, where the bodies were found, for more than six years. The house was the property of Madame L., whose mind was not strong. Witness had seen the daughter five or six times during the six years. The two lived a very quiet life, but were said to have money. Had never seen any person enter the house, except the old lady and her daughter, a tradesman once or twice, and a doctor about eight or ten times. The house was a good house – not very old. The windows were always closed, except those of the large back room on the third floor.

Isidore Musèt, policeman, said that he was called to the house at about three o'clock in the morning, and found twenty or thirty people trying to get in. Forced open the door with an iron bar. The cries continued until the door was opened – and then suddenly stopped. They seemed to be the cries of some person (or persons) in great pain – were loud and long, not short and quick. Witness led the way upstairs. On reaching the first floor, heard two voices in angry argument – one a low, rough voice, the other much higher – a very strange voice. The first voice was that of a Frenchman. Was certain that it was not a woman's voice. Could recognize several French words. The second voice – the high one – was that of a foreigner. Could not be sure whether it was the voice of a man or of a woman. Could not properly hear what was said, but believed that the language was Spanish. The state of the room and of the bodies was described by this witness as we described them yesterday.

Henri Duval, a neighbour, and by trade a metalworker, said that he was one of the party who first entered the house. Agreed with the witness, Musèt, in general. Knew

Madame L. and her daughter. Had spoken to both frequently. Was sure that the high voice was not that of either of the dead women. Thinks that it was the voice of an Italian. Was certain that it was not French. It might have been a woman's voice. Witness had no knowledge of the Italian language, but believed, by the sound, that the speaker was an Italian.

Odenheimer, restaurant keeper, a native of Holland. Not a French speaker – the following is a translation of his statement. Was passing the house at the time of the cries. They lasted for several minutes – probably ten. They were long and loud – terrible and frightening. Was one of those who entered the building. Was sure that the high voice was that of a man – of a Frenchman. Could not recognize the words spoken. They were loud and quick and spoken, it seemed, in fear as well as in anger.

Jules Mignaud, bank manager, said that Madame L'Espanaye had some property. Had opened an account at his bank eight years before. The old lady frequently paid small amounts into her account. On the third day before her death, had taken out a large sum in gold. A clerk had carried the money home for her.

Adolphe Le Bon, bank clerk, said that at midday three days before the murders, he went with Madame L'Espanaye to her house with the money from her account, contained in two bags. Mademoiselle L. opened the street door and took one of the bags from his hands. The old lady took the other. He then left. Witness did not see any person in the street at the time. It is a quiet street.

William Bird, maker of men's suits, said that he was one of the party who entered the house. Is an Englishman. Has lived in Paris for two years. Was one of the first to go up the stairs. Heard the voices in argument. The rough voice was that of a Frenchman. The high voice was very loud –

louder than the other. Is sure that it was not the voice of an Englishman. Seemed to be that of a German. Might have been a woman's voice. Witness does not understand German. Also heard the sounds of a struggle.

Four of the above-named witnesses were later questioned again. They agreed that the door of the room where the body of Mademoiselle L. was found was locked from the inside when the party reached it. Everything was perfectly silent. When the door was forced open, no person was seen. The windows, both of the back and front room, were closed and firmly locked from the inside. A door between the two rooms was shut but not locked. Another door leading from the front room into the passage was locked, with the key on the inside. A small room in the front of the house, on the third floor, at the end of the passage, was unlocked; it was full of old beds, boxes and so on. These were carefully searched. The whole house was very carefully examined. Brushes were pushed up and down the chimneys. A small door leading to the roof was nailed very firmly shut, and had clearly not been opened for years.

Alfonzo Garcio, wood worker, said that he lives in the rue Morgue. Is from Spain. Was one of the party who entered the house. Did not go upstairs. Does not like excitement. Heard the voices in argument. The low voice was that of a Frenchman. The high voice was that of an Englishman – is sure of this. Does not understand English, but judges by the rise and fall of the language.

Alberto Montani, shopkeeper, said that he was among the first to go upstairs. Heard the two voices. Recognized several words. One of the speakers was a Frenchman. The other voice spoke quickly and not clearly. Thinks it was the voice of a Russian. Witness is an Italian. Has never spoken to anyone from Russia.

Several witnesses were examined twice. They all said that

the chimneys of all the rooms on the third floor were too narrow for a human being to pass through. There is no back entrance or staircase by which anybody could have left the building while the party went up the front stairs. The body of Mademoiselle L'Espanaye was so firmly stuck in the chimney that it could not be got down until four or five of the party pulled together.

Paul Dumas, doctor, said that he was called to examine the bodies at about five o'clock in the morning. They were both then lying in the room where Mademoiselle L. was found. The body of the young lady was badly marked and cut. Witness believed that these marks and cuts, except those around the neck, were caused when the body was pushed by force up the chimney. There were clear marks of fingers on the throat. The face was pale blue in colour. The eyeballs stood out from the head. The tongue had been bitten. The stomach was discoloured. This may have been caused by the pressure of a knee. In the opinion of Monsieur Dumas, Mademoiselle L'Espanaye had been killed by pressure on the throat, which prevented her from breathing. The body of the mother was very badly damaged. All the bones on the right side of the chest were broken. A heavy bar of iron, the leg of a table, or any large, heavy weapon would have produced these results if it had been used, with great force, to attack the woman. The head of Madame L'Espanaye, when it was seen by the witness, was completely separated from the body. The throat had certainly been cut with a very sharp instrument – probably with a razor.

Nothing more of importance was discovered, although several other persons were questioned. Such a mysterious murder has never happened in Paris before – if this is a murder. The police have no idea at all where to begin.

The evening paper said that the police were holding the bank clerk, Adolphe Le Bon; but there was nothing new to report about the crime.

Dupin seemed very interested in this affair, and later that evening he spoke to me about it.

'The Paris police,' he said, 'are reasonably clever, but they do not work with a variety of methods. They search, and examine, and question as if there is only one kind of crime – and one kind of criminal – in the world. They are active and patient for a while, but when these qualities bring no results, their inquiries fail. Vidocq, for example, who used to be the Chief of Police, was a good guesser and a hard-working man. But he had never trained himself to think clearly. He believed that by having many thoughts about a problem, he was certain to arrive at the correct one. He examined a thing too closely. He would then see one or two points very clearly, but he would lose sight of the matter as a whole. Vidocq never knew when to examine a problem in a general way and when to make detailed enquiries.

'Let us look at these murders for ourselves. You will find that it can be very interesting. Besides, I know this man Le Bon. He was once very helpful to me, and I would like to help him if I can. Let us go and see this house in the rue Morgue; I would like to see it with my own eyes. We both know G——, who is still the head of the police. We shall have no difficulty in getting the necessary permission.'

When we had arranged the matter with the Chief of Police, it was still light enough for us to go immediately to the rue Morgue. We found the house easily, as there were many people looking up at it from the opposite side of the street. Before going in, we walked up the street and round to the back of the house. Dupin examined the whole neighbourhood, as well as the building itself, with the closest attention.

At last we came again to the front of the building, where we showed our letter of permission to the police officer in charge. We went upstairs – into the room where the body of Mademoiselle L'Espanaye had been found, and where both bodies still lay. Everything was as the newspaper had described it. Dupin carefully examined the room, the furniture and even the bodies. He paid particular attention to the doors and windows. We then went into the other rooms, and into the yard, and a policeman stayed with us through the whole visit. Dupin's examination lasted until it was quite dark, when we left the house. On the way home my companion called in for a moment at the office of one of the daily papers.

Typically, my friend said nothing further about the murder until midday the next day. He then asked me, suddenly, if I had noticed anything unusual at the scene of the deaths.

'No, not really,' I said; 'nothing more, that is, than we both read in the newspaper.'

'The paper,' he replied, 'has simply reported what everyone knows. It seems to me that this mystery should be easy to solve because it is extremely unusual; it is so very different from any ordinary crime. The police are confused because they can find no reason – not for the murder itself – but for the unnecessary force that was used in the murder. They are confused, too, about the voices that were heard in argument. No one was found upstairs, except the murdered woman – and there was no way of escape, except by the stairs. Then there was the body, pushed up the chimney; and the old lady's head – almost completely cut off. The police think that the unusual is necessarily a problem. But it is not. It is because many of the facts are so strange that the murder can easily be solved. The question we must ask is not "What has happened?", but "What has happened that has never happened before?"'

'I am now waiting,' Dupin went on, 'for a person who knows a great deal about these deaths, although he may not be responsible for them himself. I do not think that he is guilty of any crime. Because I believe this, I have great hopes of solving the whole problem.'

I looked at my friend in silent surprise.

'I expect to see the man here,' said Dupin, 'in this room, at any moment. If he comes, we shall have to keep him here. Take this gun; I have one too, and we both know how to use them, I think.'

I took the weapon, hardly knowing what I was doing, and Dupin continued his explanation.

'It was the voices, of course – the voices heard in argument – that gave me my first idea. All the witnesses agreed about the rough voice: it was the voice of a Frenchman. But the high voice – the high, quick one – must have been a very strange voice. An Italian, an Englishman, a Dutchman, a Spaniard and a Frenchman tried to describe it; and each one said that it sounded like the voice of a foreigner. The Italian thought it was the voice of a Russian, although he had never spoken to a Russian. The Englishman believed it to be the voice of a German, and "does not understand German". The Dutchman was sure that it was a Frenchman who spoke, but this witness needed a translator to take his statement. The Spaniard "is sure" that it was the voice of an Englishman, but "judges by the rise and fall of the language", as he "does not understand English". Our Frenchman believed that the language spoken was Spanish. Another thought that the speaker was Italian. How strange that people from five countries in Europe could recognize *nothing* familiar in that voice! It was unusual, too, that only *sounds* seem to have been made by that strange speaker; no words were recognized.

'Even before we went to the house,' said Dupin, 'I had a strong suspicion about that voice; it showed me quite clearly what I ought to look for. The next question was how the killer escaped from the building. Madame and Mademoiselle L'Espanaye were not murdered by spirits. They were murdered by beings of flesh and blood, who had somehow escaped. How? Fortunately, there is only one way of thinking about this; and it must lead us to the right answer. Let us consider, one by one, the possible means of escape. We must look only in the large back room, where the body of the daughter was found, or in the room joined to it. If the murderer had tried to escape from the third room, or from the passage, they would have been seen by the party on the stairs. The police have broken up the floors, the ceilings, and part of the walls, and have found no secret doorways. I do not trust their eyes; so I searched with my own. There was, then, no secret way out. Both doors leading to the passage were locked, with the keys on the inside. Let us consider the chimneys. These are of ordinary width for eight or ten feet above the fireplaces. But they become very narrow at the roof, and would not allow the body of a large cat to pass through. Only the windows remain. No one could have escaped through the windows of the front room without being seen by the crowd in the street. The killer must have left, then, through the windows of the back room. The police believe that this is impossible, because the windows were found closed on the inside. We know, though, that those windows are the only possible way of escape.

'There are two windows in the room. The lower part of one of them is hidden by the bed, which is pushed closely up against it. The other one is clear of all furniture, and this window was found tightly locked on the inside. Even the combined strength of several policemen failed to open it. A large hole had been made in its frame, and a thick nail was found fixed in this hole, nearly to the head. The other window showed the same sort of nail in the same sort of hole; and a determined attempt to open this window also failed. The police were now satisfied that the killer had not escaped through the windows. They therefore considered it unnecessary to take out the nails and open the windows.

'My own examination of these things was more careful – because the impossible had, in this case, to be possible. I said to myself, "The murderer *did* escape from one of these windows. But he could not have locked them again, as they were found locked from the inside. But they *were* locked. They must, then, be able to lock themselves; there is no other explanation." I went to the window that was clear of all furniture, and took out the nail. I tried to raise the window, but, as I had expected, it would not move. There must be, then, a hidden spring. After a careful search, I found it, and pressed it. There was now no need for me actually to open the window.

'I put the nail back into the hole, and looked at it carefully. A person going out through this window might have closed it after him, and the spring would have held it shut; but the nail could not have been put back. It was certain, therefore, that the killer had escaped through the other window. I climbed on the bed and examined the second window. The spring, as I had expected, was exactly the same as the first one. Then I looked at the nail. It was as thick as the other, and seemed to be fixed in the same way – driven in nearly up to the head.

'You will say that I was confused; but if you think so, you have not understood my reasoning. I could not be confused. There was no weakness anywhere in my argument. I had followed the secret to its end – and that end was the nail. It looked exactly the same as the first nail, as I say; but this fact was not at all important. The main thing was that the mystery ended here. "There must be something wrong," I said, "with the nail." I touched it; the head came off in my fingers. The rest of the nail was in the hole, where it had at some time been broken off. I put the head back in its place, and it looked exactly like a perfect nail; the broken part could not be seen. Pressing the spring, I gently raised the window slightly. The head of the nail went up with it. I closed the window, and the appearance of the whole nail was again perfect.

'The mystery, so far, was now solved. The killer had escaped through the window behind the bed. He had shut the window after him, or allowed it to shut itself, and it had locked itself. The police thought that it was the nail which held the window shut.

'The next question was how the murderer had reached the ground. Now I am sure that he entered and left the room in the same way; so let us first find out how he entered. When we walked around the building, I noticed a pipe which carries rainwater from the roof. It is about five and a half feet from the window. No one could have reached the window from the top of this pipe. But the shutter is as wide as the window – about three and a half feet – and made in the form of a single door. If this shutter were swung wide open, right back to the wall, it would reach to within two feet of the pipe. An active and courageous robber might have stretched across from the pipe and taken a firm hold of the shutter. He could then let go his hold of the pipe, and he would be hanging on the inside face of the shutter. Then, pushing with his feet against the wall, he might have swung the shutter closed. If the window was open, he could then have swung himself into the room.

'Of course a very unusual skill and courage would be needed to enter the room in this way. I have shown that it is possible, but I know that it is hardly a human possibility, Now consider carefully the very unusual activity and the very strange voice. These two features really solve the mystery for us.'

When Dupin said this, I began to understand what his idea might be; but before I could say anything, he went on with his explanation.

'It is a waste of time to look for a reason for this crime. The police are confused by the gold which was delivered to the house three days before the murders. This money was not touched by the killer; but the bank clerk who delivered it has been put in prison! It is an accident – a simple chance – that these two events happened at about the same time. Do not let the gold confuse us. Because it was not taken, we need not give it further thought.

'Now, bearing in mind the main points – the strange voice, the unusual activity and the complete absence of any reason for murder – let us consider the actual killing. Here is a woman killed by the pressure of two hands around her neck; she was then pushed up a chimney, head downwards. You must agree that this is a very strange way of hiding a body. Has anyone ever before tried to hide a body in this way? Think, too, how great must have been the strength of the killer! The body had been pushed *up* the chimney so firmly that the combined efforts of several people were needed to drag it *down*!

'Turn now to the hair – to the handfuls of thick hair which had been pulled out by the roots, and which lay in the fireplace. Great force must be used to pull out even thirty or forty hairs together; but these handfuls contained, perhaps, half a million hairs. Immense power would be necessary to pull them all out at the same time. The body of the old lady shows again what terrible strength the killer used. Her throat was not simply cut, but the head was, with one blow, almost completely cut off and the weapon was an ordinary razor.

'Of course the doctor was wrong when he said that a heavy instrument had been used on Madame L'Espanaye. Her bones were certainly broken as a result of her fall from the window on to the stone floor of the yard. The police did not think of this, because to them it is impossible that the windows were ever opened at all.

'I have in my hand the last, and perhaps the best, proof of my argument. I took these loose hairs from the tightly closed fingers of Madame L'Espanaye. Tell me what you think about them.'

'Dupin!' I said. 'This hair is most unusual – this is not human hair.'

'I did not say it was,' he replied. 'And the finger marks on the

93

throat of Mademoiselle L'Espanaye were also not human. Look here: I have copied them in this drawing, exactly as they appear on her throat. No human fingers could reach this distance from the thumb.'

I looked at the drawing, and was forced to agree with Dupin.

'Read now,' he said, 'this page from Cuvier's book on the wild animals of the East Indian Islands.'

It was a full description of a creature known as the orangutang. The great size, the strength and the behaviour of this animal, including its tendency to copy others, are well known. I understood immediately how the crime took place.

'This description of the fingers,' I said, after I had read the page, 'agrees exactly with your drawing. And the hair which you found seems to be the same as that of Cuvier's animal. An orangutang must have killed the women. But how do you explain the two voices that were heard?'

'At present I do not know who the rough voice – which was said to be the voice of a Frenchman – belongs to. But I have strong hopes of a solution. A Frenchman saw the murders; his voice was heard upstairs. If you remember, the two voices were said to be "arguing angrily". It is, I believe, very probable that the Frenchman was angry because the animal had attacked the women. The animal may have escaped from him. He may have followed it to the house, but, for some reason, could not, or did not, catch it. It may still be free – in fact, I feel sure that it is, although I cannot explain this feeling. If the Frenchman is not really guilty of these murders, he will come to this house in answer to my advertisement. You remember that I called at the office of a certain newspaper on our way home last night; I left an advertisement there. This particular newspaper prints news about the movement of ships, and it is always read by seamen.'

Dupin handed me a paper, and I read this:

CAUGHT In a Paris park, early in the morning of the —
(the morning of the murder), a very large orangutang from
Borneo. The owner (who is a sailor, belonging to a Maltese
ship), may have the animal again if he can describe it
correctly. A few small costs must be paid. Call at —, third
floor.

'How do you know,' I said, 'that the man is from a Maltese ship?'

'I do not know,' replied Dupin. I am not *sure* of it. Look at this
small piece of cloth which I found at the bottom of the pipe
behind Madame L'Espanaye's house. It is a little dirty, and I think
it has been used for tying hair up in one of those long tails which
sailors are so fond of. Also, this knot is one which few people
besides sailors can tie; and it is most common in Malta. Now, if I
am wrong about this piece of cloth, no great harm has been
done. The man will think that I have made a mistake in some
detail about the animal, and it will not trouble him. But if I am
right, a great advantage will be gained. The man will probably say
to himself. "I am not guilty of this murder. I am poor. My
orangutang is a valuable animal – to me it is worth a fortune.
Why should I lose it through a foolish fear of danger? It was
found in a park, and there are no parks near the scene of the
crime. How can anyone know that an animal killed those
women? The police have failed to solve the case. Even if they
suspect an animal, there is nothing to prove that I saw the
murder; there is nothing to prove me guilty. Above all, I am
known. The person who advertised describes me as the owner of
the animal. I am not sure how much he knows. If I do not claim
this valuable animal, people may begin to suspect something. I do
not want to call attention either to myself or to the animal. I will
visit the man, get the orangutang, and keep it shut up until this
matter has been forgotten."'

At this moment we heard a step on the stairs.

'Be ready,' said Dupin, 'with your gun, but do not use it or show it until I give a signal.'

There was a knock at the door of our room.

'Come in,' said Dupin, in a cheerful voice.

A man entered. He was a sailor, clearly – a tall, strong person, with a happy, honest expression. His face, greatly sunburnt, was more than half hidden by a beard. He had with him a heavy stick, but seemed to carry no other weapon. He wished us 'good evening' in a voice which showed that he was from Paris.

'Sit down, my friend,' said Dupin. I suppose you have called about the orangutang. He is a very fine animal, and no doubt a valuable one. How old do you say he is?'

The sailor smiled, and then replied calmly: 'I have no way of knowing – but he can't be more than four or five years old. Have you got him here?'

'Oh no; we have no place to keep him here. He is near here at a stable. You can get him in the morning. Of course, you can describe him for us – to prove that you are the owner?'

'Oh yes, sir. And I'm very happy to pay you a reward for finding the animal – that is to say, anything reasonable.'

'Well,' replied my friend, 'that is very good of you. Let me think! – what should I have? Oh! I will tell you. You must give me all the information you can about these murders in the rue Morgue.'

Dupin said the last words very quietly. Just as quietly, too, he walked towards the door, locked it, and put the key in his pocket. He then took the gun from his coat, and laid it slowly on the table.

The sailor's face grew red; he got up quickly, and took hold of his stick. The next moment he fell back into his seat, trembling violently. He said nothing. I felt very sorry for him.

'My friend,' said Dupin, in a kind voice, 'do not be afraid. We shall not harm you. I give you my word, as a gentleman, and as a Frenchman, that we do not intend to harm you. I know quite well that you are not responsible for the deaths of the two women, but it would be foolish of you to say that you know nothing about them. The position at present is this: you have done nothing which you could have avoided – nothing to bring suspicion on yourself. You did not even rob them, when you could have done so easily enough. You have nothing to hide. At the same time, you are a man of honour and so you must tell us all that you know. There is a man in prison at this moment, charged with the crime of murder; he should be set free.'

The sailor looked less anxious as Dupin said these words, although his cheerful expression had completely gone.

'With God's help,' he said after a pause, 'I will tell you all I know about this affair; but I do not expect you to believe even a half of what I say – I would be a fool if I did.'

What he told us was this. He had caught the orangutang in Borneo while he was on a journey to the East Indian Islands. With great difficulty he had brought it back to France, with the intention of selling it. He had locked it safely, as he thought, in a room at his house in Paris.

Very early on the morning of the murder, he had returned from a party to find that the animal had broken out of its room. It was sitting in front of a mirror, playing with a razor. When he saw such a dangerous weapon in the hands of such a wild animal, the man picked up a whip, which he often used to control the creature. The animal immediately rushed out of the room, down the stairs, and through an open window into the street. It was still holding the razor.

The Frenchman followed. The streets were very quiet, as it was nearly three o'clock in the morning. The man had nearly caught up with the animal, when it turned into a narrow street behind the rue Morgue. There its attention was attracted by a light shining from the open window of Madame L'Espanaye's flat. The orangutang ran to the house, saw the pipe, and climbed up with unbelievable speed. When it reached the top of the pipe, it seized the shutter, swung across to the open window and landed inside on the bed. The animal kicked the shutter open again as it entered the room. The whole movement – from the ground to the bed – did not take a minute.

The sailor had strong hopes now of catching the animal, as it could hardly escape from the building, except by the pipe. At the same time, he was troubled by what it might do in the house. After a moment he decided to follow it. Being a sailor, he had no difficulty in climbing the pipe. But when he arrived as high as the window, which was far over to his left, he could go no further. All he could do was to lean out, and watch what was happening inside the room. What he saw gave him such a shock that he nearly fell from the pipe. Madame L'Espanaye and her daughter had been sorting out some clothes from a drawer when the animal jumped on them.

The orangutang seized Madame L'Espanaye by her hair and put the razor to her face. She fought hard, and angered the creature. With one determined stroke of the razor, it nearly cut off her head. The sight of blood made the animal wild, and it fell next on the girl. Making fearful noises, it pressed its terrible fingers round her throat, and kept its hold until she died. Then the orangutang turned and saw the face of its master outside the window. Immediately its anger changed to fear – fear of the whip. It rushed around, breaking the furniture as it moved. It searched crazily for a hiding place for the bodies. First it seized the body of the girl, and pushed it up the chimney, where it was found. Then it picked up that of the old lady, and threw it straight through the open window.

The sailor, shocked beyond belief, had tried to calm the animal. His words, and the angry sounds of the animal, were heard by the people who entered the house. But he failed completely. Shaking with fear, he slid down the pipe and hurried home. He hoped that he would see no more of his orangutang.

I have hardly anything to add. The animal must have escaped from Madame L'Espanaye's flat in the way that Dupin described. It must have closed the window after it had passed through. It was later caught by the seaman himself, and sold for a large amount of money to the Paris zoo. The clerk, Le Bon, was set free at once, as soon as Dupin had explained the facts to the Chief of Police. That official found it difficult to hide his anger and shame at the result of the case. As we left his office, we heard him say that he hoped the police would, in future, be allowed to do their job without others involving themselves in police business.

Dupin did not think that a reply was necessary.

ACTIVITIES

'William Wilson' and 'The Gold-Bug'

Before you read

1 Read the Introduction to the book. What seem to be typical features of Poe's stories?

2 What do you think 'The Gold-Bug' is about? Find two meanings of the word *bug* in your dictionary.

3 Answer the questions. Find the words in *italics* in your dictionary. They are all used in the stories.
  Why might someone:
  a travel with a *companion*?
  b wear a *mask*?
  c feel *misery*?
  d be embarrassed by a *namesake*?
  e use *silk thread*?
  f look through a *telescope*?
  g *tremble*?

4 Are these statements correct? Correct the ones that are wrong.
  a A *determined* person gives up easily.
  b A *kid* is a young goat.
  c *Mercy* is an unkind act.
  d Monkeys eat *nuts*.
  e Your *skull* is part of your arm.
  f Some animals have *tales*.
  g People look for *treasure* to destroy it.

After you read

5 Discuss:
  a how the two William Wilsons are similar.
  b how they are different.
  c how the story ends. What do you think the true relationship is between the two William Wilsons?

6 Imagine you are Legrand, from 'The Gold-Bug', a few years later. Explain to a new friend how you became so wealthy.

The Fall of the House of Usher' and 'The Red Death'

Before you read

7 Discuss these questions.
  a What does the title suggest is likely to happen in 'The Fall of the House of Usher'?
  b What do you think the Red Death might be?

8 Find these words in your dictionary. Put them in the sentences below.

  disturb   immense   shield

  a It was an ..... house, with forty rooms.
  b He swung his sword but hit the other man's ....
  c Please don't ..... me while I'm working.

After you read

9 Answer the questions about 'The Fall of the House of Usher'.
  a Why has the relationship between Roderick Usher and his sister always been special?
  b How does Madeline's illness affect her?
  c What does Roderick do with his sister's body?
  d Why is Roderick so upset afterwards?
  e How do Madeline and Roderick die?
  f What happens to the house at the end?

10 Can you find a moral in 'The Red Death'? How sympathetic do you feel to the prince's behaviour?

'The Barrel of Amontillado' and 'The Whirlpool'

Before you read

11 What do you think the connection is between an expensive wine, an underground cave and a desire for revenge?

12 Find the meaning of *whirlpool* in your dictionary. What do you know about the causes and effects of whirlpools? What happens when ships get caught in them?

13 Make sentences with these pairs of words. Check their meaning in your dictionary.
  a *log, barrel*
  b *slope, horizon*

14 At the beginning of the 'The Barrel of Amontillado', Montreso describes two conditions for successful revenge. What are they Do you agree with him? Does he succeed?

15 Imagine that you are the main character in 'The Whirlpool' Describe what you saw and felt as the whirlpool pulled you down and how you saved yourself.

'The Pit and the Pendulum' and 'The Stolen Letter'

Before you read

16 Find the words *pit* and *pendulum* in your dictionary. In the first o these two stories a man is waiting to be killed. What part do you think a pit and a pendulum could play?

17 If you wanted to hide a letter in a particular room of your house and you suspected that somebody would search that room, where would you hide it?

18 Find the word *suspicion* in your dictionary. If you have a suspicion that someone is a criminal, how sure are you?

After you read

19 Discuss why 'The Pit and the Pendulum' is so frightening. Were you surprised by the ending? Would you prefer a different one?

20 Answer these questions about 'The Stolen Letter'.
   a Who has stolen the letter, from whom and why?
   b How does the policeman know that the letter is still in the thief's possession?
   c How do the police manage to search the thief's house?
   d Where has the thief actually hidden the letter?
   e What does Dupin do when he has solved the problem?

'Metzengerstein' and 'The Murders in the Rue Morgue'

Before you read

21 'Metzengerstein' is about a quarrel between two families that i passed from parents to children and on to their children. Do you know of any real or fictional situations like this one?

22 'The Murders in the Rue Morgue' is the second story in this collection about C. Auguste Dupin. What do you already know about him?

23 Find the words below in your dictionary. Which is a word for:

    a a cover for a window?

    b an animal?

    c a place where an animal is kept?

    orangutang   shutter   stable

After you read

24 Explain how and why Frederick dies in 'Metzengerstein'.

25 Write questions about 'The Murders in the Rue Morgue' to which these are the answers.

    a Madame and Mademoiselle L'Espanaye.

    b In the chimney.

    c With a razor.

    d On the inside of doors to the passage.

    e Through a window in the back room.

    f The island of Borneo.

    g By means of an advertisement.

    h To the zoo.

Writing

26 Which of the stories did you enjoy most? Which did you enjoy least? Explain why.

27 Which character were you most interested in? Explain why.

28 Choose a character from any of the stories. Imagine what happens to that character after the end of the story. Write about it.

29 Describe one of these, using your own words:

    a the House of Usher before the building is destroyed

    b the great whirlpool

    c Frederick's painting

30 Write one of these reports.

    a Imagine you are the prisoner who is saved from the Inquisition. Your report on your experiences will be used against the people who put you in the room described in the story.

b Imagine you are Roderick Usher's friend. Your report for the police explains how Roderick and Madeline died and persuades them that you were not involved in their deaths.

31 Poe describes 'a world of terror' in his stories. Describe this world.

Answers for the Activities in this book are published in our free resource packs for teachers, the Penguin Readers Factsheets, or available on a separate sheet. Please write to your local Pearson Education office or to: Marketing Department, Penguin Longman Publishing, 5 Bentinck Street, London W1M 5RN.